Real Food

FREEZER

MEALS

65 BUDGET-FRIENDLY, CLEAN EATING MAKE-AHEAD MEALS, INCLUDING WHOLE30, PALEO AND KETO COMPLIANT RECIPES

ERIN CHASE

FREE ONLINE WORKSHOP

Want to spend less time in the kitchen, and more time enjoying other things in life? Need dinner to "take care of itself"? Want to personalize and customize a freezer meal plan - with recipes your family will love?

MyFreezEasy will do all the heavy lifting for you! In a matter of seconds, our apps will pull together your freezer meal recipes, shopping lists, step-by-step instructions and printable labels for your meals. Load up your freezer with make-ahead meals and dinnertime will be a breeze.

In this free online workshop, you'll learn just about everything you need to know about freezer cooking and how it can transform your family's dinner experience.

Sign up for free at: www.myfreezeasy.com/workshop

TABLE OF CONTENTS

How Freezer Cooking
Helps Me Survive This Busy Mom Life

Freezer cooking and the "fast food at home" philosophy of MyFreezEasy has saved me from the drive thru - take out - dining out temptation on dozens (hundreds!?) of occasions! I'm not opposed to the drive thru or take out or dining out, but I do think those meals out on the town should be planned and part of your budget. Getting meals that hold up in the freezer and cook easily in the slow cooker has helped keep me out of the drive thru and eating more meals at home that are healthier and more frugal.

Recently, I found myself at the pediatrician's office with the last appointment of the day. I generally have a 'no last appointment of the morning or afternoon' policy with doctor's offices, because you end up waiting while they catch up from falling behind throughout their visits. But that was the only slot I could get that day for a son whom I suspected had strep throat.

So I'm still sitting in the waiting room at 4:50pm, waiting to see the doctor. At that point, I knew it would be 6pm before we got home, and I'm normally in the kitchen from 5 - 6 pm to prep dinner or reheat a freezer meal. That particular day, I was starting to worry. The temptation to hit the local burger joint on my way home was getting stronger. And just as I was adding up what that drive thru bill might cost, my husband texted that he was on his way home from work.

PHEW! I quickly texted back and asked if he'd be able to get dinner going in the skillet. He said he didn't have anything pressing when he got home, so I shot back the play-by-play on how to thaw and reheat some sloppy joe meat from the freezer.

When I finally arrived home after the strep test (it was positive) and buzzing through to pick up the prescription, it was 6pm. And it smelled amazing in the house, and I just scooped together some sloppy joes, cut up some fruit, grabbed some chips and dinner was served. Total cost of the meal was probably around $5-$6 for all of us. (I'm a ninja sale and deals grocery shopper!)

I was able to save dinner that night, without having to spend $40 in the drive thru!

Another example comes from this past flu season. In 2018, the flu season was exceptionally rough and it hit our family twice - once with each strain. We ended up having a sick kid home from school and activities for 7 weeks in a row, with a brief reprieve in between the 2 strains.

I did my best to keep the sick ones quarantined, keep the house clean and disinfected, plus the time and energy spent nursing them back to health - I was exhausted. There was little energy left for dinner.

It was during those weeks that we'd have back-to-back-to-back freezer meals because they require little thought and little time and little energy to get onto the table.

Another great way to make freezer to slow cooker meals work in your favor is to take a peek at your weekly schedule and figure out which day/days you need help with dinner, or which days you have activities and appointments that keep you away from home and out of the kitchen from 5-6 pm, when you would otherwise be doing meal prep. Make those your "standing freezer to slow cooker meal days."

For the past 2 years, our third son has a 5 pm every Monday appointment with the occupational therapist. Her office is about a 20 minute drive, so we are away from home from 4:30ish to 6:30ish every Monday. I'm unable to be home, in the kitchen making a 'fresh meal' for dinner, so I let the slow cooker do the hard work for me. Every-single-Monday. Without fail.

Freezer meals and specifically "freezer to slow cooker meals" play such an important role in a busy mom's kitchen. They help keep dinner on the table night after night, even when life is busy, fast, hectic and chaotic. It's such a blessing having freezer meals "on backup" for the nights each week when you need them.

They also help you stay "one step ahead" with both the prepping and the cooking. This helps keep me balanced in my mental energy, eliminating the 'what's for dinner' question, plus it helps keep me on schedule with getting dinner on the table. It's so much easier for me to punch busy in the face when I have dinner "on demand" in the freezer.

Again, the idea and goal of these types of meals is to prep make-ahead meals and keep them in your freezer, to reheat or cook them quickly at a later time. My preferred method is to double 5 recipes, which gets me 10 meals into the freezer in one session. We have built the MyFreezEasy recipes, web app and mobile apps to reflect this philosophy and strategy.

Because it really is the easiest and best way to do "fast food at home."

Before we get to the recipes, I thought I'd share some other freezer cooking hacks with you.

MyFreezEasy's freezer cooking meal plans are the perfect solution for the crazy busy home chef who wants to have less stress and less mess when getting dinner on the table.

MyFreezEasy meal plans are designed to help you get 10 meals into your freezer in under one hour, using recipes that can quickly be pulled together into freezer bags or trays. Yes, you can easily put together 10 "dump dinners" in an hour's time.

Even with the fast assembly process and cutting out the dinner hour stress, there are still a number of other essential "HACKS" for putting together MyFreezEasy recipes and meal plans.

1. Let the food cool down completely to reduce risk of freezer burn!

2. Package up and remove as much air possible, if using a plastic baggie. If using a plastic container and freezing liquid, be sure to leave enough headspace at the top, as the liquid will expand as it freezes.

3. "Flat freeze" by pressing the food as flat as possible in the baggie. Then you can stack meals and save space in your freezer. Place a torn piece of wax or parchment paper in between the baggies to prevent them from sticking together and tearing.

4. Thaw completely in the fridge overnight or for up to 2 days if it is 'thick.' If you need the food that day, or within 30 minutes, you can let it soak in a warm bowl of water and it will quickly thaw. The thickness of the baggie or container will determine how long it will take to thaw. When I 'quick-thaw' things, it can take anywhere from 20 minutes to an hour.

Note: If utilizing the quick thaw method, please don't leave raw meat out on the counter in a bowl of warm water. Always let raw meat thaw in the refrigerator to keep it at proper cold temperatures.

5. My recommended "stay in the freezer times" are: up to 6 months for regular fridge freezer, or up to 12 months in deep freezer.

6. Do not (I repeat, do NOT!) shop and prep on the same day. Find a time in your schedule that will allow you to shop the morning/afternoon/evening before, then prep the meals the following day.

7. When meat is on sale at your store, prepare the meals with a plan that will use up all the meat and you'll kill two birds with 1 stone.

- You've saved a ton by stocking up on meat that is on sale.
- You've saved a ton of time and sanity by prepping it all for dinner at once.

8. Use the "Prep Day Shopping List by Recipe" (at the back of this cookbook) when in the checkout lane (or even as you are loading and unloading your cart!) to organize ingredients into specific bags so that when you get home, the ingredients are already grouped together by recipe. The bagger might look at you like you've lost your mind, but you'll be smiling when you get home when it's already organized for your prep & assembly!

9. Drop produce and meats into the fridge in their bags so they are easy to pull out the next day when it's prep time. Leave shelf stable ingredients on the counter, ideally organized in their bags, to make prep set up a cinch.

10. Side Dishes: I leave these very much open and flexible to allow your family to decide which veggies and/or starches are best for your preferences. Make the most of sales and deals on produce and bulk rice or pasta to save big on side dishes too.

One of the keys with eating a restrictive diet like Ketogenic, Whole30 or Paleo is having your meals prepped in advance. With these kinds of diets, there is more time spent in the kitchen preparing ingredients, vegetables and proteins.

Importance of make-ahead.

Below are a few notes about these types of "Real Food Freezer Meals."

Notations

Each recipe included will contain the ⓚKeto - ⓟPaleo - ⓦ³⁰Whole30 notation for meals that are completely compliant. The main dish and what's being frozen would be compliant, as noted. Side dishes are up to you to round out and complete the perfect meal for your diet.

Special Notes

Some of the recipes in this cookbook contain special notes related to specific ingredients, substitutions, making homemade spice mixes, etc. Please know that we've pulled together the most popular, most delicious, and most freezer-friendly recipes - and it's up to you to make any specific ingredient substitutions based on your diet.

MyFreezEasy's Keto recipes

The Keto recipes in MyFreezEasy and in this cookbook are as close as we can get to the right protein, fat and veggie ratio given that it's a freezer-friendly meal. You might take a look at the ingredients and not see enough fat for you, and if that's the case...then add lots of butter to your side dishes, or to the main meal! Or balance these out with the other foods you're eating throughout the day. Also, several of the recipes in this cookbook are not marked with "Keto" because they contain fruit. You could always omit that fruit, or make adjustments if you can.

Thawing Meals

Please note the thawing instructions on any of the recipes that include seafood, or recipes that are grilled. Spoiler alert: we recommend that you thaw these meals COMPLETELY before cooking them. Seafood is tender and delicate and you don't want to overcook it because you had to bake it longer while it defrosted and then cooked. Also, meats that are grilled should be thawed completely so they will cook through evenly, and not dry out.

Compliant ingredients

Please read the directions closely to ensure that the ingredients you use are compliant with your diet. You might need to make adjustments with sweeteners, or make up a homemade spice mix or sauce, depending on the meal.

Compliant side dishes

MyFreezEasy's recipes and freezer-friendly meals call for most of the ingredients going into the freezer. With each meal, we recommend different side dishes that would pair well with that meal. In this cookbook, many of those side dishes are veggies, salads with compliant vinaigrette, cauliflower rice, riced broccoli, zoodles (zucchini noodles.) You are welcome to mix up the side dishes, based on what you prefer, what's on sale at your grocery store, and what you have on hand. We leave the side dishes up to your preferences and creative genius!

And with that, let's move onto the delicious recipes!

Chapter 1 - Baked Recipes

Bacon Meatloaf
Baked Tomato-Basil Tilapia {Foil Packs}
Baked Lemon & Dill Salmon
Firecracker Pork Chops
Basil Balsamic Chicken
Baked Italian Pork Chops
Cuban Style Pork Chops
Chipotle Pork Chops
Garlic Lime Chicken
Greek Chicken Bake
Sesame Ginger Salmon
Pollo Asado
Mediterranean Salmon
Lemon Garlic Roasted Chicken
Lemon Dijon Salmon
Italian Stuffed Zucchini Boats

Bacon Meatloaf

Yield: 4 servings
Prep Time: 15 minutes
Cook Time: 60 minutes

Ingredients

- 2 lbs. lean ground beef
- 1 Tbsp minced onion
- 1 tsp garlic powder
- 1/2 cup almond flour
- 1 egg
- 12 slices bacon
- Side: salad
- 1 - 9x5 disposable foil loaf pan

Cooking Directions

1. Preheat the oven to 350 F.
2. In a large mixing bowl, combine the ground beef, minced onion, garlic powder, almond flour, egg and mix well.
3. Line the meatloaf pan with bacon, so the ends touch in the middle of the base of the pan and the bacon lays to the outside of the pan. You want the bacon to wrap around to the top of the meatloaf. Press the meatloaf mixture into the pan, then wrap the bacon pieces around the meatloaf.
4. Bake in the preheated oven for 55 to 60 minutes, or until beef is cooked in the middle and the bacon is crispy on top. If you need to crisp up the bacon, run it under the broiler for 1-2 minutes.
5. Prepare the salad.
6. Serve Bacon Meatloaf with salad.

Prepare to Freeze Directions

- In a large mixing bowl, combine 2 lbs. ground beef, 1 Tbsp minced onion, 1/2 tsp garlic powder, 1/2 cup almond flour, 1 egg and mix well.
- To the disposable loaf tray, add the following ingredients:
  - 12 slices of bacon, set up to wrap around the beef
  - Prepared meatloaf
- Cover with foil or lid, add label and freeze.

Freeze & Thaw Directions

Put tray in the freezer and freeze up to 6 months in fridge freezer or 12 months in a deep freezer. Thaw completely in the fridge overnight, or a warm shallow dish of water for about 20 minutes, before transferring to the oven and baking as directed.

Baked Tomato-Basil Tilapia {Foil Packs}

Yield: 4 servings
Prep Time: 10 minutes
Cook Time: 15 minutes

Ingredients

- 4 tilapia fillets
- 4 tsp olive oil
- Salt and pepper
- 8 oz. cherry tomatoes
- 1 bunch fresh basil
- Side: cauliflower rice
- Side: salad
- Foil
- 1 gallon-size freezer baggie

Cooking Directions

1. Preheat the oven to 400 F.
2. Halve all the cherry tomatoes. Chiffonade the basil.
3. Place each tilapia fillet on a piece of foil large enough to wrap around the fillet. To each fillet, add 1 tsp olive oil, salt and pepper. Evenly divide the halved tomatoes and basil into each foil pack. Wrap the foil up into packs.
4. Bake in the preheated oven for 10 to 15 minutes, or until tilapia is cooked through. Cooking time may vary, depending on thickness of the tilapia.
5. Cook the cauliflower rice, as directed.
6. Prepare the salad.
7. Serve Baked Tomato-Basil Tilapia with cauliflower rice and salad.

Prepare to Freeze Directions

- Halve the cherry tomatoes. Chiffonade basil.
- Set up 4 large pieces of foil.
- To each piece of foil, add the following ingredients:
  - 1 tilapia fillet
  - 1 tsp olive oil
  - Salt and pepper
  - Halved cherry tomatoes, evenly divided among the packs
  - Basil shreds, evenly divided among the packs
- Wrap foil tightly around the tilapia and veggies. Place foil packs into a gallon-size plastic freezer baggie. Add label to baggie and freeze.

Freeze & Thaw Directions

Put baggie in the freezer and freeze up to 6 months in fridge freezer or 12 months in a deep freezer. Thaw completely in the fridge before baking as directed.

Baked Lemon & Dill Salmon

Yield: 4 servings
Prep Time: 10 minutes
Cook Time: 20 minutes

Ingredients

- 1 lb. salmon fillet
- Salt and pepper
- 2 small lemons
- 2 tsp fresh dill
- Side: veggies
- Side: riced broccoli
- 1 gallon-size freezer baggie

Cooking Directions

1. Preheat oven to 350 F. Lightly grease a 7x11 or 9x13-inch baking dish with non-stick cooking spray.
2. Slice lemons in half. Finely chop the fresh dill.
3. Place the 4 salmon fillets into the baking dish, skin side down. Sprinkle each with little salt and pepper over the top. Drizzle juice from the lemon halves over the salmon pieces. Then, slice the squeezed lemon halves and place on top of the salmon. Place fresh chopped dill sprigs on salmon.
4. Bake in the preheated oven for 15 to 20 minutes, or until salmon is cooked through. Cooking time will vary depending on thickness of the salmon fillets.
5. Cook riced broccoli, as directed on package.
6. Prepare veggies.
7. Serve Lemon & Dill Salmon with cauliflower riced broccoli and veggies.

Prepare to Freeze Directions

- Cut 1 lb. salmon into 4 - 1/4 lb. fillets.
- Slice 2 lemons.
- Finely chop 2 tsp fresh dill.
- To gallon-size plastic freezer baggie, add the following ingredients:
  - Salmon fillets
  - Salt and pepper
  - Lemon slices
  - Chopped dill
- Remove as much air as possible and seal. Add label to baggie and freeze.

Freeze & Thaw Directions

Put baggie in the freezer and freeze up to 6 months in fridge freezer or 12 months in a deep freezer. Thaw completely in the fridge overnight, or a warm bowl of water for about 20 minutes, before transferring to baking dish and baking at 350 F for 20 minutes, or until salmon is cooked through.

Firecracker Pork Chops

Yield: 4 servings
Prep Time: 10 minutes
Cook Time: 40 minutes

Ingredients

- 1 tsp paprika
- 1 Tbsp chili powder
- 1 tsp garlic powder
- 1 tsp onion powder
- 1/2 tsp crushed red pepper
- 4 boneless pork chops
- Salt and pepper
- Side: cauliflower rice
- Side: veggies
- 1 gallon-size freezer baggie

Cooking Directions

1. Preheat the oven to 350 F. Lightly spray a 9×13-inch glass baking dish with non-stick cooking spray.
2. In a small mixing bowl, combine the paprika, chili powder, garlic powder, onion powder and crushed red pepper. Sprinkle a little of the dry rub into the base of the prepared baking dish and place the pork chops and rub into the dry rub in the baking dish. Then sprinkle a little salt and pepper over the pork chops.
3. Press the rest of the dry rub onto the top of the pork chops, coating them well.
4. Bake in the preheated oven for 25 to 40 minutes, depending on the thickness of the chops. Let rest 5 minutes before serving. (Thinner chops can take as little as 25 minutes, and thicker chops up to 40 minutes. Bake until internal temperature reaches 145 F.)
5. Cook the cauliflower rice, as directed.
6. Prepare veggies.
7. Serve Firecracker Pork Chops with rice and veggies.

Prepare to Freeze Directions

- In a small bowl, mix up the rub for both meals by combining 1 tsp paprika, 1 Tbsp chili powder, 1 tsp garlic powder,1 tsp onion powder and 1/2 tsp crushed red pepper.
- To gallon-size plastic freezer baggie, add the following ingredients:
  - Boneless pork chops
  - Salt and pepper
  - Prepared spice mix, rubbed onto the pork chops in each bag
- Remove as much air as possible and seal. Add label to baggie and freeze.

Freeze & Thaw Directions

Put baggie in the freezer and freeze up to 6 months in fridge freezer or 12 months in a deep freezer. Thaw in a warm bowl of water for about 20 minutes, before transferring to the baking dish and baking as directed.

Basil Balsamic Chicken

Yield:	4 servings
Prep Time:	15 minutes*
Cook Time:	60 minutes

Ingredients

- 4 small boneless, skinless chicken breasts
- 1/2 cup balsamic vinegar
- 2 Tbsp olive oil
- Salt and pepper
- 2 tsp dried basil
- Side: cauliflower rice
- Side: veggies
- 1 gallon-size freezer baggie

Cooking Directions

1. Place the chicken into a bowl or dish and add the balsamic vinegar and olive oil. Season lightly with salt and pepper.* Let marinate in the fridge for at least 30 minutes...ideally overnight!
2. Preheat oven to 350 F. Lightly grease a baking dish with non-stick cooking spray.
3. Place the marinated chicken in the baking dish and generously sprinkle the basil on top. Bake for an hour, or until the chicken has cooked through. Cooking time may vary depending on thickness of the chicken pieces. Slice the chicken and divide into 4 portions.
4. Cook the cauliflower rice, as directed.
5. Serve Basil Balsamic Chicken with cauliflower rice and veggies.

Prepare to Freeze Directions

- To gallon-size plastic freezer baggie, add the following ingredients:
  - 4 small boneless, skinless chicken breasts
  - 1/2 cup balsamic vinegar
  - 2 Tbsp olive oil
  - Salt and pepper
  - 2 tsp dried basil
- Remove as much air as possible and seal. Add label to baggie and freeze.

Freeze & Thaw Directions

Put baggie in the freezer and freeze up to 6 months in fridge freezer or 12 months in a deep freezer. Thaw in the fridge overnight, or a warm bowl of water for about 20 minutes, before transferring to baking dish and baking as directed. If baking from partially frozen, cover with foil and increase bake time by 1.5 or 2 times the listed baking time.

Baked Italian Pork Chops

Yield: 4 servings
Prep Time: 10 minutes
Cook Time: 30 minutes

(K) (P) (W30)

Ingredients

- 4 boneless pork chops
- Salt and pepper
- 15 oz. can diced tomatoes
- 1 Tbsp Italian seasoning
- 1 tsp minced garlic
- 1 tsp minced onion
- Side: cauliflower rice
- Side: salad
- 1 - 9x13 disposable foil tray

Cooking Directions

1. Preheat the oven to 400 F.
2. Place the pork chops into baking dish and sprinkle with salt and pepper.
3. Open and drain the diced tomatoes.
4. In a small mixing bowl, stir together the drained diced tomatoes, Italian seasoning, minced garlic and minced onion. Pour tomato-spice mixture on top of the pork chops.
5. Bake in the preheated oven for 25 to 30 minutes, or until pork chops are cooked through. Cooking time may vary depending on thickness of the chops.
6. Prepare the salad.
7. Prepare the cauliflower rice.
8. Serve Baked Italian Pork Chops with salad and cauliflower rice.

Prepare to Freeze Directions

- Open and drain 1 can of diced tomatoes.
- In a small mixing bowl, stir together the can of drained diced tomatoes, 1 Tbsp Italian seasoning, 1 tsp minced garlic, and 1 tsp minced onion.
- To each disposable tray, add the following ingredients:
  - 4 boneless pork chops
  - Salt and pepper
  - Diced tomatoes-spices mixture
- Cover with foil or lid, add label and freeze.

Freeze & Thaw Directions

Put tray in the freezer and freeze up to 6 months in fridge freezer or 12 months in a deep freezer. Thaw in the fridge overnight, or a warm shallow dish of water for about 20 minutes, before transferring to the oven and baking as directed. If baking from partially frozen, cover with foil and increase bake time by 1.5 or 2 times the listed baking time.

Cuban Style Pork Chops

Yield: 4 servings
Prep Time: 10 minutes
Cook Time: 40 minutes

Ingredients

- 4 boneless pork chops
- Salt and pepper
- 1/4 cup orange juice
- 3 Tbsp lime juice
- 2 tsp minced garlic
- 2 tsp paprika
- 1 tsp dried oregano
- 1 tsp onion powder
- 1 tsp ground cumin
- Side: riced broccoli
- Side: veggies
- 1 gallon-size freezer baggie

Cooking Directions

1. Lightly spray a 9x13-inch baking dish with non-stick cooking spray. Place the pork chops into the baking dish and season both sides with salt and pepper.
2. In a small mixing bowl, whisk together the orange juice, lime juice, minced garlic, paprika, dried oregano, onion powder and ground cumin. Pour the marinade over the pork chops and marinate in the fridge for at least 30 minutes.
3. Cook the riced broccoli, as directed.
4. Preheat oven to 375 F.
5. Once marinated, bake the pork chops in the preheated oven for 30 to 40 minutes, or until pork chops reach 145 F. Let rest for 5 minutes before serving or slicing. Cooking time may vary depending on thickness of the pork chops.
6. Prepare veggies.
7. Serve Cuban Style Pork Chops over riced broccoli with veggies.

Prepare to Freeze Directions

- In a small mixing bowl, whisk together 1/4 cup orange juice, 3 Tbsp lime juice, 2 tsp minced garlic, 1 tsp paprika, 1 tsp dried oregano, 1 tsp onion powder, and 1 tsp ground cumin.
- To gallon-size plastic freezer baggie, add the following ingredients:
  - 4 boneless pork chops
  - Salt and pepper
  - Prepared marinade
- Remove as much air as possible and seal. Add label to baggie and freeze.

Freeze & Thaw Directions

Put baggie in the freezer and freeze up to 6 months in fridge freezer or 12 months in a deep freezer. Thaw in the fridge overnight, or a warm bowl of water for about 20 minutes, before transferring to the baking dish and baking as directed. If baking from partially frozen, cover with foil and increase bake time by 1.5 or 2 times the listed baking time.

Chipotle Pork Chops

Yield: 4 servings
Prep Time: 5 minutes
Cook Time: 35 minutes

Ingredients

- 4 boneless pork chops
- Salt and pepper
- 15 oz. can diced tomatoes
- 1 tsp minced garlic
- 1 tsp ground cumin
- 1 tsp chipotle chili powder
- Side: cauliflower rice
- Side: veggies
- 1 gallon-size freezer baggie

Cooking Directions

1. Preheat oven to 350 F. Place the pork chops into small baking dish and season both sides with salt and pepper.
2. In a mixing bowl, toss together the diced tomatoes with minced garlic, ground cumin and chipotle chili powder. Pour the tomatoes over the pork chops and bake in the preheated oven for 30 to 35 minutes, or until pork is cooked through. Let rest 5 minutes before serving.
3. Prepare veggies.
4. Prepare the cauliflower rice.
5. Serve Chipotle Pork Chops with cauliflower rice and veggies.

Prepare to Freeze Directions

- Open the can diced tomatoes.
- In a mixing bowl, toss together 1 can diced tomatoes with 1 tsp minced garlic, 1 tsp ground cumin and 1 tsp chipotle chili powder.
- To gallon-size plastic freezer baggie, add the following ingredients:
  - 4 boneless pork chops
  - Salt and pepper
  - Diced tomatoes and seasoning mixture
- Remove as much air as you can and seal. Freeze up to 6 months in your fridge freezer or 12 months in a deep freezer.

Freeze & Thaw Directions

Put baggie in the freezer and freeze up to 6 months in fridge freezer or 12 months in a deep freezer. Thaw in the fridge overnight, or a warm bowl of water for about 20 minutes, before transferring to the baking dish and baking as directed. If baking from partially frozen, cover with foil and increase bake time by 1.5 or 2 times the listed baking time.

Garlic Lime Chicken

Yield: 4 servings
Prep Time: 10 minutes
Cook Time: 35 minutes

Ingredients

- 4 small boneless, skinless chicken breasts
- 1/4 cup lime juice
- 1/4 cup olive oil
- 1 Tbsp minced garlic
- Salt and pepper
- Side: cauliflower rice
- Side: salad
- 1 gallon-size freezer baggie

Cooking Directions

1. In a mixing bowl, whisk together the lime juice, olive oil, minced garlic, salt and pepper. Add the chicken breasts and coat with the marinade. Place in the fridge and let marinate for at least 2 hours.
2. Preheat oven to 350 F.
3. Place the chicken and marinade into baking dish and bake in the preheated oven for 35 minutes, or until chicken is cooked through. If desired, run under the broil for 2 minutes to crisp up the tops of the chicken.
4. Cook the cauliflower rice, as directed.
5. Prepare the salad.
6. Serve Garlic Lime Chicken over cauliflower rice with salad.

Prepare to Freeze Directions

- To gallon-size plastic freezer baggie, add the following ingredients:
    - 4 small boneless, skinless chicken breasts
    - 1/4 cup lime juice
    - 1/4 cup olive oil
    - 1 Tbsp minced garlic
    - Salt and pepper
- Remove as much air as possible and seal. Add label to baggie and freeze.

Freeze & Thaw Directions

Put baggie in the freezer and freeze up to 6 months in fridge freezer or 12 months in a deep freezer. Thaw in the fridge overnight, or a warm bowl of water for about 20 minutes. Transfer the chicken and marinade to baking dish and bake as directed. If baking from partially frozen, cover with foil and increase bake time by 1.5 or 2 times the listed baking time.

Greek Chicken Bake

Yield: 4 servings
Prep Time: 10 minutes
Cook Time: 45 minutes

Ingredients

- 4 small boneless, skinless chicken breasts
- Salt and pepper
- 2 cups cherry tomatoes
- 1 cup artichoke hearts
- 1 cup green olives
- 2 Tbsp olive oil
- 2 Tbsp lemon juice
- 2 tsp minced garlic
- 2 tsp dried oregano
- Garnish: feta cheese crumbles
- Side: salad
- 1 - 9x13 disposable foil tray

Cooking Directions

1. Preheat the oven to 400 F.
2. Drain the artichoke hearts, pat dry, and then quarter them.
3. In a small mixing bowl, whisk together the olive oil, lemon juice, minced garlic and oregano.
4. Place the chicken breasts into a 9x13-inch baking dish and sprinkle with a little salt and pepper. Add the cherry tomatoes, quartered artichoke hearts and olives around the chicken pieces. Pour the lemon juice marinade over the top.
5. Bake in the preheated oven for 45 minutes, or until chicken is cooked through. Sprinkle Feta cheese crumbles onto warm chicken bake, so they soften up. Omit garnish if Whole30/Paleo.
6. Prepare the salad.
7. Serve Greek Chicken Bake with salad.

Prepare to Freeze Directions

- In a small mixing bowl, whisk together the 2 Tbsp olive oil, 2 Tbsp lemon juice, 2 tsp minced garlic and 2 tsp oregano.
- Drain 1 cup artichoke hearts, pat dry and then quarter them.
- To disposable foil tray, add the following ingredients:
  - 4 small boneless, skinless chicken breasts
  - Salt and pepper
  - Cherry tomatoes
  - Quartered artichoke hearts
  - Green olives
  - Prepared Greek lemon marinade
- Cover tightly with foil or lid, add label to tray and freeze.

Freeze & Thaw Directions

Put tray in the freezer and freeze up to 6 months in fridge freezer or 12 months in a deep freezer. Thaw in the fridge overnight, or a warm shallow dish of water for about 20 minutes, before transferring to the oven and baking as directed. If baking from partially frozen, cover with foil and increase bake time by 1.5 or 2 times the listed baking time.

Special Note: *Omit the Feta cheese crumbles for Whole30 & Paleo meal.*

Sesame Ginger Salmon

Yield:	4 servings
Prep Time:	10 minutes
Cook Time:	20 minutes

Ingredients

- 1/4 cup olive oil
- 2 Tbsp gluten-free soy sauce or coconut aminos
- 2 Tbsp rice vinegar
- 2 Tbsp sesame oil
- 2 Tbsp honey or compliant sweetener
- 2 garlic cloves
- 1 tsp ground ginger
- 1 Tbsp sesame seeds
- 2 green onions
- 1 lb. salmon fillet, divided into 1/4 lb pieces
- Side: cauliflower rice
- Side: veggies
- 1 gallon-size freezer baggie

Cooking Directions

1. Place the salmon fillet pieces into small baking dish.
2. In a medium bowl, whisk together olive oil, soy sauce or coconut aminos, rice vinegar, sesame oil, honey or compliant sweetener, garlic, ginger, sesame seeds and green onions. Pour over the salmon. Let marinate for at least 30 minutes in the fridge.
3. Preheat oven to 400 F. Bake the salmon and marinade for 20 minutes, or until the fish flakes easily with a fork.
4. Cook cauliflower rice, as directed.
5. Prepare veggies.
6. Serve Sesame Ginger Salmon with cauliflower rice and veggies.

Prepare to Freeze Directions

- Slice 2 green onions.
- Crush 2 cloves of garlic.
- In a medium bowl, whisk together 1/4 cup olive oil, 2 Tbsp soy sauce or coconut aminos, 2 Tbsp rice vinegar, 2 Tbsp sesame oil, 2 Tbsp honey or compliant sweetener, 2 crushed garlic cloves, 1 tsp ground ginger, 1 Tbsp sesame seeds and sliced green onions.
- To gallon-size plastic freezer baggie, add the following ingredients:
  - 4 salmon fillets
  - Prepared marinade
- Remove as much as air as possible and seal.

Freeze & Thaw Directions

Put baggie in the freezer and freeze up to 6 months in fridge freezer or 12 months in a deep freezer. Thaw completely in the fridge overnight, or a warm bowl of water for about 20 minutes, before transferring to the baking dish to cook.

Pollo Asado

Yield: 4 servings
Prep Time: 10 minutes*
Cook Time: 40 minutes

Ingredients

- 1 lb. boneless, skinless chicken thighs
- Salt and pepper
- 3 Tbsp olive oil
- 1/2 cup orange juice
- 1 lime
- 1 lemon
- 1 tsp oregano
- 1 tsp ground cumin
- 1 tsp paprika
- 4 garlic cloves
- 1/2 small red onion
- Side: cauliflower rice
- Side: veggies
- 1 gallon-size freezer baggie

Cooking Directions

1. Add the chicken thighs to a shallow baking dish or small roasting pan and sprinkle salt and pepper over the chicken.
2. In a mixing bowl, add the olive oil, orange juice, juice from lime, juice from lemon, oregano, ground cumin and paprika. Add the crushed garlic cloves and red onion, then whisk well. Pour the marinade over the chicken in the shallow dish. *Let marinate for at least 30 minutes in the fridge.
3. Preheat oven to 400 F.
4. Roast the marinated chicken for 35 to 40 minutes, or until golden brown on top and chicken is cooked through. Cooking time may vary depending on thickness of the chicken.
5. Cook the cauliflower rice, as directed.
6. Prepare veggies.
7. Serve Pollo Asado with cauliflower rice and veggies.

Prepare to Freeze Directions

- Halve 1 lemon and 1 lime.
- Finely chop 1/2 small red onion. Crush 4 cloves of garlic.
- In a mixing bowl, add 3 Tbsp olive oil, 1/2 cup orange juice, juice from lime, juice from lemon, 1 tsp oregano, 1 tsp ground cumin and 1 tsp paprika. Add the 4 crushed garlic cloves and chopped red onion. Whisk well.
- To gallon-size plastic freezer baggie, add the following ingredients:
  ◦ 1 lb. boneless, skinless chicken thighs
  ◦ Salt and pepper
  ◦ Marinade
- Remove as much as air as possible and seal.

Freeze & Thaw Directions

Put baggie in the freezer and freeze up to 6 months in fridge freezer or 12 months in a deep freezer. Thaw in the fridge overnight, or a warm bowl of water for about 20 minutes, before transferring to baking dish or roasting pan and baking as directed. If baking from partially frozen, cover with foil and increase bake time by 1.5 or 2 times the listed baking time.

Mediterranean Salmon

Yield: 4 servings
Prep Time: 5 minutes
Cook Time: 20 minutes

Ingredients

- 1 lb. salmon fillet
- Salt and pepper
- 1 pint cherry tomatoes
- 6 oz. can sliced black olives
- 2 Tbsp capers
- 1 tsp dried oregano
- Side: salad
- Side: cauliflower rice
- 1 gallon-size freezer baggie

Cooking Directions

1. Cook cauliflower rice, as directed.
2. Preheat oven to 400 F.
3. Halve the cherry tomatoes. Open and drain the can of black olives.
4. Cut salmon fillet into 4 pieces. Place in small baking dish and season with salt and pepper. Add the halved cherry tomatoes, sliced black olives, capers and oregano over and around the salmon.
5. Bake in the preheated oven for 15 to 20 minutes, or until salmon is no longer pink in the middle.
6. Prepare the salad.
7. Serve Mediterranean Salmon with side of cauliflower rice and salad.

Prepare to Freeze Directions

- Cut 1 lb. of salmon fillet into 4 pieces.
- Halve 1 pint of cherry tomatoes.
- Open and drain a can of black olives.
- To gallon-size plastic freezer baggie, add the following ingredients:
    - 4 salmon pieces
    - Salt and pepper
    - Halved cherry tomatoes
    - 6 oz. can sliced black olives
    - 2 Tbsp capers
    - 1 tsp dried oregano
- Remove as much air as possible and seal. Add label to baggie and freeze.

Freeze & Thaw Directions

Put baggie in the freezer and freeze up to 6 months in fridge freezer or 12 months in a deep freezer. Thaw completely in the fridge overnight, or a warm bowl of water for about 20 minutes, before transferring the salmon and toppings to baking dish. Bake at 400 F for 15 to 20 minutes.

Lemon Garlic Roasted Chicken

Yield: 4 servings
Prep Time: 15 minutes
Cook Time: 45 minutes

Ingredients

- 4 small boneless, skinless chicken breasts
- Salt and pepper
- 8 garlic cloves
- 2 lemons
- 2 Tbsp olive oil
- 2 Tbsp lemon juice
- 2 tsp dried oregano
- Side: salad
- Side: zoodles
- 1 - 9x13 disposable foil tray

Cooking Directions

1. Thinly slice the lemons. Peel and smash the garlic cloves with the side of a knife to crack them open.
2. Preheat the oven to 400 F.
3. In a small mixing bowl, whisk together the olive oil, lemon juice, and oregano.
4. Place the chicken breasts into a 9x13-inch baking dish and sprinkle with a little salt and pepper. Add the lemon slices and smashed garlic cloves around the chicken pieces. Pour the lemon juice marinade over the top.
5. Bake in the preheated oven for 45 minutes, or until chicken is cooked through.
6. Prepare the salad.
7. Cook the zoodles as directed.
8. Serve Lemon Garlic Roasted Chicken with salad and zoodles.

Prepare to Freeze Directions

- Thinly slice 2 lemons. Peel and smash 8 garlic cloves with the side of a knife, to crack them open.
- In a small mixing bowl, whisk together the 2 Tbsp olive oil, 2 Tbsp lemon juice and 2 tsp oregano.
- To gallon-size plastic freezer baggie, add the following ingredients:
  ○ 4 small boneless, skinless chicken breasts
  ○ Salt and pepper
  ○ Lemon slices
  ○ Smashed garlic cloves
  ○ Prepared lemon juice marinade
- Cover with foil or lid, add label and freeze.

Freeze & Thaw Directions

Put tray in the freezer and freeze up to 6 months in fridge freezer or 12 months in a deep freezer. Thaw in the fridge overnight, or a warm shallow dish of water for about 20 minutes, before transferring to the oven and baking as directed. If baking from partially frozen, cover with foil and increase bake time by 1.5 or 2 times the listed baking time.

Lemon Dijon Salmon

Yield: 4 servings
Prep Time: 10 minutes
Cook Time: 20 minutes

Ingredients

- 1 lb. salmon fillet
- 1/4 cup lemon juice
- 1 Tbsp Dijon mustard
- 1 Tbsp fresh parsley
- Salt and pepper
- Side: spinach salad & compliant vinaigrette
- Side: cauliflower rice
- 1 gallon-size freezer baggie

Cooking Directions

1. Preheat the oven to 400 F.
2. Cook cauliflower rice, as directed.
3. Chop the parsley.
4. In a small mixing bowl, whisk together the lemon juice, Dijon mustard and chopped parsley.
5. Place the salmon fillet or pieces into small baking dish and pour the lemon marinade over the top. Sprinkle with salt and pepper.
6. Bake in the preheated oven for 15 to 20 minutes, or until salmon is flaky and cooked through.
7. Prepare spinach salad with compliant vinaigrette.
8. Serve Lemon Dijon Salmon with cauliflower rice and spinach salad.

Prepare to Freeze Directions

- Cut salmon into 4 pieces, if needed.
- Chop 1 Tbsp parsley.
- In a small mixing bowl, whisk together 1/4 cup lemon juice, 1 Tbsp Dijon mustard and 1 Tbsp chopped parsley.
- To gallon-size plastic freezer baggie, add the following ingredients:
  ○ 4 salmon pieces
  ○ Lemon marinade
  ○ Salt and pepper
- Remove as much air as possible and seal. Add label to baggie and freeze.

Freeze & Thaw Directions

Put baggie in the freezer and freeze up to 6 months in fridge freezer or 12 months in a deep freezer. Thaw completely in the fridge overnight, or a warm bowl of water for about 20 minutes, before transferring to baking dish and baking at 400 F for 15 to 20 minutes.

Italian Stuffed Zucchini Boats

Yield: 4 servings
Prep Time: 20 minutes
Cook Time: 20 minutes

Ingredients

- 4 large zucchini
- 1 lb. ground beef
- 1 red bell pepper
- 1 Tbsp minced onion
- 1 tsp garlic powder
- 1 cup marinara sauce
- Salt and pepper
- 1 cup Parmesan cheese
- Garnish: fresh basil
- Side: salad
- 1 - 9x13 disposable foil tray

Cooking Directions

1. Preheat the oven to 350 F.
2. Bring large pot of water to boiling. Slice the zucchini in half, lengthwise. Once boiling, place the zucchini flesh-side down into the boiling water and boil for 2 minutes. Remove and repeat until all zucchini halves are boiled. Place on paper towel to drain and pat dry. Using a melon baller or spoon, scoop out the flesh of the zucchini and place into baking dish.
3. Seed and chop the red bell pepper.
4. In a large skillet, brown the ground beef with the chopped red bell pepper, minced onion and garlic powder. Once browned, drain and then stir in the marinara sauce. Let simmer for a few minutes.
5. Spoon the beef sauce into the zucchinis and top with Parmesan cheese (omit if Paleo/Whole30.) Bake in the preheated oven for 15 to 20 minutes.
6. Prepare the salad.

7. Serve Italian Stuffed Zucchini Boats with basil garnish and side salad.

Prepare to Freeze Directions

- Bring large pot of water to boiling. Slice the zucchini in half, lengthwise. Once boiling, place the zucchini flesh-side down into the boiling water and boil for 2 minutes. Remove and repeat until all zucchini halves are boiled. Place on paper towel to drain and pat dry. Using a melon baller or spoon, scoop out the flesh of the zucchini and place into baking dish.
- Seed and chop 1 red bell peppers.
- Brown 1 lb. ground beef with the chopped red bell peppers, 1 Tbsp minced onion and 1 tsp garlic powder. Drain and then stir in 1 cup marinara sauce.
- To each disposable tray, add the following ingredients:
  ○ Boiled and dried zucchini
  ○ Beef-marinara sauce
  ○ 1 cup Parmesan cheese, sprinkled on top
- Cover with foil or lid, add label and freeze.

Freeze & Thaw Directions

Put tray in the freezer and freeze up to 6 months in fridge freezer or 12 months in a deep freezer. Thaw in the fridge overnight, or a warm shallow dish of water for about 20 minutes, before transferring to the oven and baking as directed.

Special Note: *Omit the Parmesan cheese for Paleo or Whole30 compliant meal. Check marinara sauce for hidden sugars and carbs.*

Chapter 2 - Grill Recipes

Grilled Apple Juice Brined Pork Chops

Grilled Citrus Salmon Packs

Grilled Greek Chicken Kebabs

Grilled Lemon Avocado Chicken

Grilled Pork Chops with Zucchini & Tomatoes

Grilled Pork Chops, Peaches & Red Onions

Grilled Southwest Chicken

Grilled Southwest Pork Chops

Grilled Southwestern Steaks

Grilled Spice-Rubbed Pork Chops

Grilled Tilapia with Pineapple Salsa

Grilled Tomato-Basil Tilapia {Foil Packs}

Garlic Chicken Kebabs

Grilled Mango & Red Bell Pepper Chicken {Foil Packs}

Apple Juice Brined Pork Chops

Yield: 4 servings
Prep Time: 10 minutes*
Cook Time: 10 minutes

Ingredients

- 4 boneless pork chops
- 1 cup apple juice
- 2 Tbsp salt
- 2 cups water
- Side: salad
- Side: zoodles
- 1 gallon-size freezer baggie

Cooking Directions

1. Place apple juice, salt, and 2 cups of water into shallow dish. Place pork chops into the brine in single layer and pour enough water over the top so the pork chops are covered.* Cover with foil and refrigerate for at least 2 hours.
2. Once finished, brining, drain the liquid and pat the pork chops dry. Grill or saute the pork chops for 4 to 5 minutes per sid, or until cooked through. Cooking time may vary depending on thickness of pork chops.
3. Prepare the salad.
4. Cook the zoodles as directed.
5. Serve Apple Juice Brined Pork Chops with salad and zoodles.

Prepare to Freeze Directions

- In a small mixing bowl, stir together 1 cup apple juice, 2 Tbsp salt and 2 cups water.
- To gallon-size plastic freezer baggie, add the following ingredients:
  - 4 boneless pork chops
  - Apple juice brine
- Remove as much air as you can and seal. Freeze up to 6 months in your fridge freezer or 12 months in a deep freezer.

Freeze & Thaw Directions

Put baggie in the freezer and freeze up to 6 months in fridge freezer or 12 months in a deep freezer. Thaw in the fridge overnight, or a warm bowl of water for about 20 minutes, before transferring to grill and grilling as directed.

Grilled Citrus Salmon Packs

Yield: 4 servings
Prep Time: 10 minutes
Cook Time: 15 minutes

Ingredients

- 1 lb. salmon fillet
- 1 tsp dried dill
- Salt and pepper
- 1 lemon
- 1 lime
- 1 orange
- Side: spinach salad
- Side: veggies
- 4 pieces foil
- 1 gallon-size freezer baggie

Cooking Directions

1. Place each salmon fillet in a piece of foil that is about 10 to 12 inches long or large enough to wrap around the salmon and fruit to make a "packet."
2. Slice the lemon, lime and orange, into at least 4 slices of each.
3. Generously season the salmon with dill, salt and pepper. Top each fillet with a slice of lemon, lime and orange. Wrap the foil, creating a packet, and place on the grill.
4. Grill for 15 minutes, or until salmon has cooked through. Cooking time will vary on thickness of the fillet and heat of the grill.
5. Prepare the spinach salad with compliant vinaigrette.
6. Prepare veggies.
7. Serve Grilled Citrus Salmon with spinach salad and veggies.

Prepare to Freeze Directions

- Cut 1 lb. salmon into 4 - 1/4 lb. fillets & remove skin.
- Set up 4 large pieces of foil.
- Thinly slice 1 lemon, 1 lime and 1 orange.
- To each piece of foil, add the following ingredients:
  - 1 salmon fillet
  - Sprinkle of dill, salt and pepper
  - 1 slice each of the lemon, lime and orange
- Wrap each foil sheet around the salmon and fruit to create a pack. Place the packs into the gallon size freezer baggie. Remove as much as air as possible and seal.

Freeze & Thaw Directions

Put baggie in the freezer and freeze up to 6 months in fridge freezer or 12 months in a deep freezer. Thaw completely before placing salmon packs onto the grill and grill for 15 minutes, or until salmon is cooked through.

Grilled Greek Chicken Kebabs

Yield: 4 servings
Prep Time: 20 minutes*
Cook Time: 15 minutes

Ingredients

- 1/4 cup olive oil
- 1/4 cup lemon juice
- 2 tsp oregano
- Salt and pepper
- 2 large boneless, skinless chicken breasts
- 1 small red onion
- 1 red bell pepper
- 1 small zucchini
- 18 whole green or black olives
- Side: salad
- 1 - 9x13 disposable foil tray

Cooking Directions

1. In a large bowl, add the olive oil, lemon juice, oregano and salt and pepper.* Mix in the chicken and let marinate for at least 30 minutes in the fridge, tossing every 10 minutes.
2. Cut up the veggies and set them out to string the skewers.
3. Once the chicken has marinated, thread the chicken pieces, red onion pieces, bell pepper pieces, zucchini pieces and olives onto skewers.
4. Grill for 10-15 minutes, rotating 2 or 3 times, until chicken is cooked through and veggies have softened. Grilling time may vary depending on heat on the grill and size of the chicken pieces.
5. Prepare side salad.
6. Serve Grilled Greek Chicken Kebabs with simple side salad.

Prepare to Freeze Directions

- Cut 4 boneless, skinless chicken breasts into bite size pieces.
- Cut 1 red onions into 1-inch pieces. Cut 1 red bell peppers into 1-inch pieces. Slice 1 zucchini into 1/2-inch medallions.
- Whisk 1/4 cup olive oil, 1/2 cup lemon juice, 2 tsp oregano and salt and pepper. Mix in the chicken pieces from 4 chicken breasts and let marinate in the fridge for 30 minutes.
- Thread the chicken pieces, red onion pieces, bell pepper pieces, zucchini pieces and olives onto skewers.
- Add prepared kebabs to disposable foil tray.
- Cover tightly with foil or lid, add label to tray and freeze.

Freeze & Thaw Directions

Put trays in the freezer and freeze up to 6 months in fridge freezer or 12 months in a deep freezer. Thaw completely in the fridge before grilling as directed.

Lemon Avocado Chicken

Yield: 4 servings
Prep Time: 10 minutes*
Cook Time: 15 minutes

Ingredients

- 4 small boneless, skinless chicken breasts
- 1/2 cup water
- 2 Tbsp salt
- 2 lemons, divided
- 2 tsp minced garlic
- 1 avocado
- 2 Tbsp cilantro
- Salt and pepper
- Side: salad
- Side: cauliflower rice
- 1 gallon-size freezer baggie

Cooking Directions

1. In a large mixing bowl, whisk together the water, salt, juice from the lemon and the minced garlic. Slice the lemon and add to the brine. *Place the chicken breasts into the brine and let soak for at least 30 minutes, in the fridge.
2. Prepare the cauliflower rice.
3. Preheat the grill. Pull the chicken breasts out of the brine and pat dry. Discard brine.
4. Grill over direct heat for 4 to 6 minutes per side, until cooked through. Grilling time may vary depending on the thickness of the chicken.
5. While the chicken is grilling, add the avocado, juice from 1 lemon and chopped cilantro to small food processor and puree. Use avocado sauce as garnish or dip for the grilled chicken.
6. Prepare the salad.
7. Serve Lemon Avocado Chicken with cauliflower rice and salad.

Prepare to Freeze Directions

- To gallon-size plastic freezer baggie, add the following ingredients:
  - 4 small boneless, skinless chicken breasts
  - 1/2 cup water
  - 2 Tbsp salt
  - 1 lemon, sliced
  - 2 tsp minced garlic
- Remove as much air as possible and seal. Add label to baggie and freeze.

Freeze & Thaw Directions

Put baggie in the freezer and freeze up to 6 months in fridge freezer or 12 months in a deep freezer. Thaw completely in the fridge overnight, or a warm bowl of water for about 20 minutes, before transferring to the grill and grilling as directed. Prepare the avocado sauce while chicken is grilling.

Grilled Pork Chops with Zucchini & Tomatoes

Yield: 4 servings
Prep Time: 10 minutes
Cook Time: 25 minutes

Ingredients

- 4 boneless pork chops
- 8 oz. cherry tomatoes
- 2 small zucchini
- 1 small red onion
- 2 Tbsp olive oil
- Salt and pepper
- Side: zoodles
- 1 gallon-size freezer baggie
- 1 quart-size freezer baggie

Cooking Directions

1. In a large bowl, toss tomatoes, zucchini, onion, olive oil, and salt and pepper to taste. Set aside.
2. Preheat the grill.
3. Place the vegetables in a grill basket and grill, turning or tossing occasionally, until crisp-tender and lightly charred, 8 to 10 minutes.
4. Season pork chops with salt and pepper on both sides, and then grill until internal temperature reaches 145 degrees F, about 4 1/2 minutes per side. Remove chops from grill and let rest 3 minutes.
5. Remove vegetables and cover to keep warm while chops rest.
6. Cook the zoodles as directed.
7. Serve Grilled Pork Chops with Zucchini & Tomatoes with zoodles.

Prepare to Freeze Directions

- Slice 2 small zucchini into 1-inch pieces. Cut 1 red onions into 1-inch pieces.
- In a large bowl, toss 8 oz cherry tomatoes, sliced zucchini, diced red onions, 2 Tbsp olive oil, and salt and pepper to taste. Mix together and then place in 1 quart size freezer baggie.
- To gallon-size plastic freezer baggie, add the following ingredients:
  ° 4 boneless pork chops
  ° Salt and pepper on each side
  ° Quart size baggie with the zucchini and tomatoes
- Remove as much air as possible and seal. Add label to baggie and freeze.

Freeze & Thaw Directions

Put baggie in the freezer and freeze up to 6 months in fridge freezer or 12 months in a deep freezer. Remove the veggie pack from the baggie and thaw in the fridge. Thaw the pork chops in the fridge completely before grilling.

Grilled Pork Chops, Peaches & Red Onions

Yield: 4 servings
Prep Time: 10 minutes
Cook Time: 15 minutes

Ingredients

- 4 small boneless pork chops
- 1/2 tsp garlic powder
- 1/2 tsp onion powder
- Salt and pepper
- 4 large peaches
- 1 medium red onion
- Side: riced broccoli
- Side: salad
- 1 gallon-size freezer baggie

Cooking Directions

1. Season the pork chops with garlic powder, onion powder and salt and pepper. Grill the pork chops for 5 to 6 minutes on each side, or until internal temperature reaches 145 F. Grilling time will vary depending on heat of the grill and thickness of the chop.
2. Halve the peaches and lay them flesh side down on the grill. Lay the red onion rings on the grill and grill peaches and red onions for 6 to 8 minutes, flipping the red onions once.
3. Cook the riced broccoli, as directed.
4. Prepare salad.
5. Serve Grilled Pork Chops, Peaches & Red Onions with riced broccoli and salad.

Prepare to Freeze Directions

- Slice 1 red onion into onion-ring like circles.
- Seed and halve 4 peaches.
- To gallon-size plastic freezer baggie, add the following ingredients:
  - 4 boneless pork chops
  - 1/2 tsp garlic powder
  - 1/2 tsp onion powder
  - Salt and pepper
  - Peach halves
  - Red onion slices
- Remove as much as air as possible and seal.

Freeze & Thaw Directions

Put baggie in the freezer and freeze up to 6 months in fridge freezer or 12 months in a deep freezer. Thaw completely before grilling pork chops alongside the peaches and red onions. Grill as directed.

Grilled Southwest Chicken

Yield: 4 servings
Prep Time: 10 minutes
Cook Time: 15 minutes

Ingredients

- 4 small boneless, skinless chicken breasts
- 1 Tbsp canola oil
- 1 Tbsp chili powder
- 1 tsp ground cumin
- 1 tsp crushed red pepper
- 1 tsp garlic powder
- Salt and pepper
- Side: cauliflower rice
- Side: salad
- 1 gallon-size freezer baggie

Cooking Directions

1. In a small mixing bowl, stir together the canola oil, chili powder, ground cumin, crushed red pepper and garlic powder. Add a pinch of salt and pepper.
2. Place chicken breasts into a baking dish and spread the spice mix onto both sides of the chicken breasts. Let marinate for at least 30 minutes in the fridge.
3. Preheat the grill.
4. Grill for 5 to 6 minutes per side, over direct heat, or until cooked to 145 F. Cooking time may vary depending on thickness of the chicken.
5. Cook the cauliflower rice, as directed.
6. Prepare salad.
7. Serve Grilled Southwest Chicken with cauliflower rice and salad.

Prepare to Freeze Directions

- In a small mixing bowl, stir together the 1 Tbsp canola oil, 1 Tbsp chili powder, 1 tsp ground cumin, 1 tsp crushed red pepper and 1 tsp garlic powder. Add a pinch of salt and pepper.
- To gallon-size plastic freezer baggie, add the following ingredients:
  - 4 boneless, skinless chicken breasts
  - Salt and pepper
  - Press the prepared rub onto each chicken breast
- Remove as much as air as possible and seal.

Freeze & Thaw Directions

Put baggie in the freezer and freeze up to 6 months in fridge freezer or 12 months in a deep freezer. Thaw completely in the fridge overnight, or a warm bowl of water for about 20 minutes, before transferring to grill and grilling as directed.

Grilled Southwest Pork Chops

Yield: 4 servings
Prep Time: 10 minutes
Cook Time: 15 minutes

Ingredients

- 4 boneless pork chops
- 1 Tbsp canola oil
- 1 Tbsp chili powder
- 1 tsp ground cumin
- 1 tsp crushed red pepper
- 1 tsp garlic powder
- Salt and pepper
- Side: zoodles
- Side: salad
- 1 gallon-size freezer baggie

Cooking Directions

1. In a small mixing bowl, stir together the canola oil, chili powder, ground cumin, crushed red pepper and garlic powder. Add a pinch of salt and pepper.
2. Place pork chops into a baking dish and spread the spice mix onto both sides of the pork chops. Let marinate for at least 30 minutes in the fridge.
3. Preheat the grill.
4. Grill for 5 to 6 minutes per side, over direct heat, or until cooked to 145 F. Cooking time may vary depending on thickness of the chops. Let rest 5 minutes before serving and slicing.
5. Cook the zoodles, as directed.
6. Prepare salad.
7. Serve Grilled Southwest Pork Chops with zoodles and salad.

Prepare to Freeze Directions

- In a small mixing bowl, stir together the 1 Tbsp canola oil, 1 Tbsp chili powder, 1 tsp ground cumin, 1 tsp crushed red pepper and 1 tsp garlic powder. Add a pinch of salt and pepper.
- To gallon-size plastic freezer baggie, add the following ingredients:
  - 4 boneless pork chops
  - Salt and pepper
- Press the prepared rub onto each pork chops
- Remove as much as air as possible and seal.

Freeze & Thaw Directions

Put baggie in the freezer and freeze up to 6 months in fridge freezer or 12 months in a deep freezer. Thaw completely in the fridge overnight, or a warm bowl of water for about 20 minutes, before transferring to grill and grilling as directed.

Grilled Southwestern Steaks

Yield: 4 servings
Prep Time: 10 minutes
Cook Time: 15 minutes

Ingredients

- 4 small steaks
- 1/4 cup lime juice
- 2 Tbsp olive oil
- 3 tsp chili powder
- 2 tsp minced garlic
- 1 tsp crushed red pepper flakes
- Salt and pepper
- Side: avocado
- Side: cauliflower rice
- 1 gallon-size freezer baggie

Cooking Directions

1. Add the steaks to a shallow baking dish.
2. In a small bowl, whisk together the lime juice, olive oil, chili powder, minced garlic, crushed red pepper flakes and some salt and pepper. Pour over the steak and let marinate in the fridge for at least 30 minutes.
3. Cook the cauliflower rice, as directed.
4. Grill the marinated steaks for 5 minutes on each side, or until cooked to desired temperature.
5. Slice avocados.
6. Serve Grilled Southwestern Steaks with cauliflower rice and avocado.

Prepare to Freeze Directions

- In a small bowl, whisk together 1/4 cup lime juice, 2 Tbsp olive oil, 3 tsp chili powder, 2 tsp minced garlic, 1 tsp crushed red pepper flakes and some salt and pepper.
- To gallon-size plastic freezer baggie, add the following ingredients:
  ◦ 4 steaks
  ◦ Prepared marinade
- Remove as much air as possible and seal. Add label to baggie and freeze.

Freeze & Thaw Directions

Put baggie in the freezer and freeze up to 6 months in fridge freezer or 12 months in a deep freezer. Thaw completely in the fridge before grilling the steaks.

Grilled Spice-Rubbed Pork Chops

Yield: 4 servings
Prep Time: 10 minutes
Cook Time: 15 minutes

Ingredients

- 4 boneless pork chops
- 1 tsp garlic powder
- 1 tsp onion powder
- 1 tsp ground cumin
- 1 tsp chili powder
- 1 tsp paprika
- 1 tsp honey or compliant sweetener
- 1/2 tsp salt
- 1/2 tsp pepper
- 1 cup compliant BBQ sauce
- Side: cauliflower rice
- Side: salad
- 1 gallon-size freezer baggie

Cooking Directions

1. In a small mixing bowl, toss together the garlic powder, onion powder, ground cumin, chili powder, paprika, honey or compliant sweetener, salt and pepper.
2. Place pork chops into a baking dish and press the spice rub into both sides of the pork chops.
3. Preheat the grill.
4. Grill for 5 to 6 minutes per side, over direct heat, or until cooked to 145 F. Cooking time may vary depending on thickness of the chops. Let rest 5 minutes before serving and slicing.
5. Prepare salad.
6. Cook the cauliflower rice, as directed.
7. Serve Grilled Spice-Rubbed Pork Chops with compliant BBQ sauce, cauliflower rice, and salad.

Prepare to Freeze Directions

- In a small mixing bowl, toss together 1 tsp garlic powder, 1 tsp onion powder, 1 tsp ground 1 tsp cumin, 1 tsp chili powder, 1 tsp paprika, 1 tsp honey or compliant sweetener, 1/2 tsp salt and 1/2 tsp pepper.
- To gallon-size plastic freezer baggie, add the following ingredients:
  - 4 boneless pork chops
  - Prepared rub, pressed into both sides of the pork chops
- Remove as much as air as possible and seal.

Freeze & Thaw Directions

Put baggie in the freezer and freeze up to 6 months in fridge freezer or 12 months in a deep freezer. Thaw completely in the fridge overnight, or a warm bowl of water for about 20 minutes, before transferring to grill and grilling as directed.

Special Note: *Omit the brown sugar or use compliant sweetener, also use compliant BBQ sauce.*

Grilled Tilapia with Pineapple Salsa

Yield: 4 servings
Prep Time: 10 minutes*
Cook Time: 15 minutes

Ingredients

- 4 small tilapia fillets
- Salt and pepper
- 2 Tbsp lime juice
- 1 Tbsp canola oil
- Dash cayenne pepper
- 2 cups fresh pineapple chunks
- 2 Tbsp sliced green onions
- 1 Tbsp chopped cilantro
- 1 Tbsp lime juice
- Side: riced broccoli
- Side: salad
- 1 gallon-size freezer baggie

Cooking Directions

1. In a small mixing bowl, whisk together 2 Tbsp lime juice, canola oil, cayenne pepper and a few pinches of salt and pepper.
2. Place tilapia fillets into a baking dish and brush the lime marinade onto each fillet.* Marinate for at least 30 minutes in the fridge.
3. Cook the riced broccoli, as directed.
4. Preheat the grill.
5. Grill for 2 to 3 minutes per side, over direct heat, or until cooked through and flaky. Cooking time may vary depending on thickness of the fillets.
6. Chop the fresh pineapple and toss with sliced green onions, cilantro and 1 Tbsp of lime juice.
7. Prepare salad.
8. Serve Grilled Tilapia with Pineapple Salsa topping and side of riced broccoli and salad.

Prepare to Freeze Directions

- In a small mixing bowl, whisk together 2 Tbsp lime juice, 1 Tbsp canola oil, dash of cayenne pepper and a few pinches of salt and pepper.
- To gallon-size plastic freezer baggie, add the following ingredients:
  - 4 tilapia fillets
  - Prepared marinade, brushed onto the fillets
- Remove as much as air as possible and seal.

Freeze & Thaw Directions

Put baggie in the freezer and freeze up to 6 months in fridge freezer or 12 months in a deep freezer. Thaw completely in the fridge overnight, or a warm bowl of water for about 20 minutes, before transferring to grill and grilling as directed.

Grilled Tomato-Basil Tilapia {Foil Packs}

Yield: 4 servings
Prep Time: 10 minutes
Cook Time: 20 minutes

Ingredients

- 4 tilapia fillets
- 4 tsp olive oil
- Salt and pepper
- 8 oz. cherry tomatoes
- 1 bunch fresh basil
- Side: zoodles
- Side: salad
- 4 pieces foil
- 1 gallon-size freezer baggie

Cooking Directions

1. Preheat grill.
2. Halve all the cherry tomatoes. Chiffonade the basil.
3. Place each tilapia fillet on a piece of foil large enough to wrap around the fillet. To each fillet, add 1 tsp olive oil, salt and pepper. Evenly divide the halved tomatoes and basil into each foil pack. Wrap the foil up into packs.
4. Grill around 400 F for 15 to 20 minutes, or until tilapia is cooked through. Cooking time may vary, depending on thickness of the tilapia and heat of the grill.
5. Cook the zoodles, as directed.
6. Prepare the salad.
7. Serve Grilled Tomato-Basil Tilapia with zoodles and salad.

Prepare to Freeze Directions

- Halve all 8 oz. of cherry tomatoes. Chiffonade 1 bunch of basil.
- Set up 4 large pieces of foil.
- To each piece of foil, add the following ingredients:
  - 1 tilapia fillet
  - 1 tsp olive oil
  - Salt and pepper
  - Halved cherry tomatoes, evenly divided among the packs
  - Basil shreds, evenly divided among the packs
- Wrap foil tightly around the tilapia and veggies. Place foil packs into a gallon-size plastic freezer baggie. Add label to baggie and freeze.

Freeze & Thaw Directions

Put baggie in the freezer and freeze up to 6 months in fridge freezer or 12 months in a deep freezer. Thaw completely in the fridge before grilling as directed.

Garlic Chicken Kebabs

Yield: 4 servings
Prep Time: 20 minutes*
Cook Time: 15 minutes

Ingredients

- 3 Tbsp olive oil
- 3 Tbsp lemon juice
- 3 Tbsp minced garlic
- 2 tsp oregano
- Salt and pepper
- 2 boneless, skinless chicken breasts
- 1 small red onion
- 1 red bell pepper
- 1 small zucchini
- Side: salad
- 1 - 9x13 disposable foil tray

Cooking Directions

1. Cut the chicken into 1-inch or bite size pieces.
2. In a large bowl, add the olive oil, lemon juice, minced garlic, oregano and salt and pepper. *Mix in the chicken and let marinate for at least 30 minutes in the fridge, tossing every 10 minutes.
3. Cut up the veggies into chunks and set them out to string the skewers.
4. Once the chicken has marinated, thread the chicken pieces, red onion pieces, bell pepper pieces, and zucchini pieces onto skewers.
5. Preheat the grill.
6. Grill for 10-15 minutes, rotating 2 or 3 times, until chicken is cooked through and veggies have softened. Grilling time may vary depending on heat on the grill and size of the chicken pieces.
7. Prepare side salad.
8. Serve Garlic Chicken Kebabs with side salad.

Prepare to Freeze Directions

- Cut 2 boneless, skinless chicken breasts into bite size pieces.
- Cut 1 red onion into 1-inch pieces. Cut 1 red bell pepper into 1-inch pieces. Slice 1 zucchini into 1/2-inch medallions.
- Whisk 3 Tbsp olive oil, 3 Tbsp lemon juice, 3 Tbsp minced garlic, 2 tsp oregano and salt and pepper. Mix in the chicken pieces from 4 chicken breasts and let marinate in the fridge for 30 minutes.
- Thread the chicken pieces, red onion pieces, bell pepper pieces, and zucchini pieces onto skewers.
- Add prepared kebabs to disposable foil tray.
- Brush marinade over tops and into tray
- Cover tightly with foil or lid, add label to tray and freeze.

Freeze & Thaw Directions

Put trays in the freezer and freeze up to 6 months in fridge freezer or 12 months in a deep freezer. Thaw completely in the fridge before grilling.

Grilled Mango & Red Bell Pepper Chicken {Foil Packs}

Yield: 4 servings
Prep Time: 10 minutes
Cook Time: 20 minutes

Ingredients

- 4 small boneless, skinless chicken breasts
- Salt and pepper
- 8 Tbsp lime juice
- 8 tsp olive oil
- 2 tsp ground ginger
- 2 mangos
- 2 red bell peppers
- 20 oz. can mandarin oranges
- Salt and pepper
- Side: salad
- 4 pieces foil
- 1 gallon-size freezer baggie

Cooking Directions

1. Preheat grill.
2. Place each chicken breast on a piece of foil, large enough to wrap around the chicken. Season each with salt and pepper.
3. In a small mixing bowl, whisk together the lime juice, olive oil and ground ginger. Evenly divide and pour over each chicken piece.
4. Seed and dice the mango. Seed and dice the bell pepper.
5. Open and drain the mandarin oranges.
6. Evenly divide the mango chunks, bell pepper chunks and mandarin oranges to each foil pack. Wrap tightly and seal.
7. Grill around 400 F for 15 to 20 minutes, or until chicken is cooked through. Cooking time may vary, depending on thickness of the chicken and heat of the grill. Be careful when opening, as hot steam will escape the foil pack.
8. Prepare the salad.
9. Serve Mango & Red Bell Pepper Chicken {Foil Packs} with salad.

Prepare to Freeze Directions

- Seed and dice 2 mangoes. Seed and dice 2 red bell peppers.
- In a small mixing bowl, whisk together 8 Tbsp lime juice 8 Tbsp olive oil and 2 tsp ground ginger.
- Set up 4 large pieces of foil.
- Open and drain 1 can of mandarin oranges.
- To each piece of foil, add the following ingredients:
  - 1 chicken breast
  - Salt and pepper dusting
  - Evenly divided portion of lime marinade
  - Evenly divided portion of diced mango
  - Evenly divided portion of diced red bell peppers
  - Evenly divided portion of mandarin oranges
- Wrap foil tightly around the chicken and veggies. Place all foil packs into gallon-size plastic freezer baggie. Add label to baggie and freeze.

Freeze & Thaw Directions

Put baggie in the freezer and freeze up to 6 months in fridge freezer or 12 months in a deep freezer. Thaw completely in the fridge before grilling as directed.

Chapter 3 - Slow Cooker Recipes

Slow Cooker Asian Chicken Lettuce Wraps

Yield:	4 servings
Prep Time:	10 minutes
Cook Time:	8 hours in slow cooker

Ingredients

- 4 small boneless, skinless chicken breasts
- 6 Tbsp gluten-free soy sauce or coconut aminos
- 2 Tbsp honey or other compliant sweetener
- 1 Tbsp rice vinegar
- 2 tsp minced garlic
- 1 tsp ground ginger
- 1/2 tsp crushed red pepper
- 2 Tbsp almond or coconut flour, thickener
- 16 large lettuce leaves
- Garnish: sesame seeds
- Garnish: sliced green onions
- Side: cauliflower rice
- 1 gallon-size freezer baggie

Cooking Directions

1. In a small mixing bowl, whisk together the gluten-free soy sauce or coconut aminos, honey or other compliant sweetener, rice vinegar, minced garlic, ground ginger and crushed red pepper.
2. Place the chicken breasts in the base of the slow cooker and pour the Asian sauce over the top.
3. Set on low and cook for 8 hours. With 30 minutes left in the cooking cycle, make a slurry with the almond or coconut flour and equal amount of water, and then stir it into the sauce. Cook for 30 more minutes to allow sauce to thicken.
4. Shred the chicken with 2 forks and mix into the thickened sauce. Spoon the shredded chicken into large lettuce leaves. Add the sesame seed and sliced green onions, and then wrap up the lettuce leaves.
5. Cook the cauliflower rice, as directed.
6. Serve Slow Cooker Asian Chicken Lettuce Wraps with cauliflower rice.

Prepare to Freeze Directions

- To gallon-size plastic freezer baggie, add the following ingredients:
  - 4 small boneless, skinless chicken breasts
  - 6 Tbsp gluten-free soy sauce or coconut aminos
  - 2 Tbsp honey or other compliant sweetener
  - 1 Tbsp rice vinegar
  - 2 tsp minced garlic
  - 1 tsp ground ginger
  - 1/2 tsp crushed red pepper
- Do NOT add the almond or coconut flour to freezer bag.
- Remove as much air as possible and seal. Add label to baggie and freeze.

Freeze & Thaw Directions

Put baggie in the freezer and freeze up to 6 months in fridge freezer or 12 months in a deep freezer. Thaw in the fridge overnight, or a warm bowl of water for about 20 minutes, before transferring to the slow cooker and cooking on low for 8 hours. Thicken with almond or coconut flour at the end of the cooking cycle as directed. Assemble lettuce wraps as directed.

Slow Cooker Beef Roast and Brussels Sprouts

Yield: 4 servings
Prep Time: 10 minutes
Cook Time: 8 hours in slow cooker

Ingredients

- 2 lb. beef chuck roast
- Salt and pepper
- 4 whole carrots
- 1 small yellow onion
- 20 Brussels sprouts
- 1 tsp minced garlic
- 1 cup beef broth
- 2 Tbsp coconut flour, optional
- Side: salad
- 1 gallon-size freezer baggie

Cooking Directions

1. Peel and cut the whole carrots into 1-inch pieces. Dice the yellow onion into 1/2-inch pieces.
2. Place the beef roast into the base of the slow cooker and season with salt and pepper. Sprinkle the carrot pieces, onion pieces, Brussels sprouts, minced garlic and beef broth over the roast.
3. Set the slow cooker on low and cook for 8 hours. Once finished cooking, slice the beef or shred the beef with 2 forks and mix into the sauce. Spoon out the vegetables onto serving plates. If desired, make gravy with gluten-free flour or coconut flour (keto).
4. Prepare salad.
5. Serve Slow Cooker Beef Roast and Brussels Sprouts with side salad.

Prepare to Freeze Directions

- Peel and cut 4 whole carrots into 1-inch pieces. Dice 1 small yellow onion into 1/2-inch pieces.
- To gallon-size plastic freezer baggie, add the following ingredients:
  - 2 lb. beef chuck roast
  - Salt and pepper
  - Carrot pieces
  - Diced onion
  - 20 Brussels Sprouts
  - 1 tsp minced garlic
  - 1 cup beef broth
- Remove as much air as possible and seal. Add label to baggie and freeze.

Freeze & Thaw Directions

Put baggie in the freezer and freeze up to 6 months in fridge freezer or 12 months in a deep freezer. Thaw in the fridge overnight, or a warm bowl of water for about 20 minutes, before transferring to the slow cooker and cooking on low for 8 hours.

Slow Cooker Chicken & Mushrooms

Yield: 4 servings
Prep Time: 10 minutes
Cook Time: 8 hours in slow cooker

Ingredients

- 4 small boneless, skinless chicken breasts
- 8 oz. sliced white mushrooms
- 1 small white onion
- 2 tsp minced garlic
- 1 cup chicken stock
- Salt and pepper
- 2 Tbsp almond or coconut flour, thickener
- Garnish: fresh parsley
- Side: zoodles
- Side: veggies
- 1 gallon-size freezer baggie

Cooking Directions

1. Chop the onion.
2. Place the chicken breasts in the base of the slow cooker and pour the sliced mushrooms and chopped onion around the chicken. Add the minced garlic, chicken stock and season with a little salt and pepper.
3. Set on low and cook for 8 hours. With 30 minutes left in the cooking cycle, make a slurry with the almond or coconut flour and equal amount of water, and then stir it into the sauce. Cook for 30 more minutes to allow sauce to thicken.
4. Cook the zoodles, as directed.
5. Prepare veggies.
6. Serve Slow Cooker Chicken & Mushrooms and parsley garnish with veggies and zoodles.

Prepare to Freeze Directions

- Chop 1 small white onions.
- To gallon-size plastic freezer baggie, add the following ingredients:
  - 4 small boneless, skinless chicken breasts
  - 8 oz. sliced mushrooms
  - Chopped onions
  - 2 tsp minced garlic
  - 1 cup chicken stock
  - Salt and pepper
  - Do NOT add the almond or coconut flour to freezer bag.
- Remove as much air as possible and seal. Add label to baggie and freeze.

Freeze & Thaw Directions

Put baggie in the freezer and freeze up to 6 months in fridge freezer or 12 months in a deep freezer. Thaw in the fridge overnight, or a warm bowl of water for about 20 minutes, before transferring to the slow cooker and cooking on low for 8 hours. Thicken with almond or coconut flour at the end of the cooking cycle as directed.

Slow Cooker Chicken Cacciatore

Yield: 4 servings
Prep Time: 10 minutes
Cook Time: 8 hours in slow cooker

Ingredients

- 4 small boneless, skinless chicken breasts
- Salt and pepper
- 1/4 cup compliant red cooking wine
- 1 small white onion
- 1 green bell pepper
- 1 red bell pepper
- 28 oz. can crushed tomatoes
- 2 tsp Italian seasoning
- Side: zoodles
- Side: salad
- 1 gallon-size freezer baggie

Cooking Directions

1. Slice the onion. Seed and slice the bell peppers.
2. Place the chicken breasts in the base of the slow cooker and season with salt and pepper. Add red cooking wine around the chicken. Add the sliced onion and bell peppers over the top of the chicken. Then pour the crushed tomatoes over the top and add Italian seasoning.
3. Set slow cooker on low and cook for 8 hours.
4. Cook the zoodles, as directed.
5. Prepare the salad.
6. Serve Slow Cooker Chicken Cacciatore over zoodles with salad.

Prepare to Freeze Directions

- Slice 1 small white onions. Seed and slice 1 green and 1 red bell peppers.
- Open the can of crushed tomatoes.
- To gallon-size plastic freezer baggie, add the following ingredients:
  ○ 4 small boneless, skinless chicken breasts
  ○ Salt and pepper
  ○ 1/4 cup compliant red cooking wine
  ○ Sliced onions
  ○ Sliced red and green bell peppers
  ○ Canned crushed tomatoes
  ○ 2 tsp Italian seasoning
- Remove as much air as possible and seal. Add label to baggie and freeze.

Freeze & Thaw Directions

Put baggie in the freezer and freeze up to 6 months in fridge freezer or 12 months in a deep freezer. Thaw in the fridge overnight, or a warm bowl of water for about 20 minutes, before transferring to the slow cooker and cooking on low for 8 hours.

Slow Cooker Chicken No-Tortilla Soup

Yield: 4 servings
Prep Time: 10 minutes
Cook Time: 8 hours in slow cooker

Ingredients

- 4 small boneless, skinless chicken breasts
- 1 red bell pepper
- 15 oz. can tomato sauce
- 15 oz. can petite diced tomatoes
- 1 Tbsp chili powder
- 1 tsp ground cumin
- 1 tsp garlic powder
- 1 tsp onion powder
- 2 cups chicken or vegetable stock
- Salt and pepper
- Garnish: avocado slices
- Garnish: shredded Mexican blend cheese
- Side: salad or veggies
- 1 gallon-size freezer baggie

Cooking Directions

1. Seed and dice the red bell pepper.
2. To the slow cooker, add the chicken, tomato sauce, diced tomatoes, chili powder, cumin, garlic powder, onion powder, red bell pepper, and chicken or vegetable stock. Set slow cooker on low and cook for 8 hours.
3. Before serving, use 2 forks to pull the chicken apart in the soup. Then ladle soup into bowls and add the avocado slices into each bowl. Top with shredded cheese (omit if Paleo or Whole30.)
4. Serve Slow Cooker Chicken No-Tortilla Soup with salad or veggies.

Prepare to Freeze Directions

- Seed and dice 1 red bell pepper.
- Open the can of tomato sauce.
- Open the can of diced tomatoes.
- To gallon-size plastic freezer baggie, add the following ingredients:
  - 4 small boneless, skinless chicken breasts
  - Diced red bell pepper
  - Diced tomatoes
  - Tomato sauce
  - 1 Tbsp chili powder
  - 2 cups chicken or vegetable stock
  - 1 tsp ground cumin
  - 1 tsp garlic powder
  - 1 tsp onion powder
- Remove as much air as possible and seal. Add label to baggie and freeze.

Freeze & Thaw Directions

Put baggie in the freezer and freeze up to 6 months in fridge freezer or 12 months in a deep freezer. Thaw in the fridge overnight, or a warm bowl of water for about 20 minutes, before transferring to the slow cooker and cooking on low for 8 hours. Once cooked, shred the chicken into the soup, ladle into bowls and garnish.

Special Note: *Omit cheese garnish for Whole30 & Paleo compliant meal.*

Slow Cooker Coconut Lime Chicken

Yield:	4 servings
Prep Time:	10 minutes
Cook Time:	8 hours in slow cooker

Ingredients

- 4 small boneless, skinless chicken breasts
- 1 Tbsp olive oil
- 1 red bell pepper
- 1/2 small red onion
- 1 cup chicken stock
- 2 Tbsp lime juice
- 1 cup canned coconut milk
- Garnish: chopped cilantro
- Garnish: crushed red pepper
- Side: salad
- 1 gallon-size freezer baggie

Cooking Directions

1. Cut the chicken breasts into bite-size pieces.
2. Seed and finely chop the red bell pepper. Chop the red onion.
3. Add the chicken pieces, chopped red bell peppers, chopped red onions, chicken stock, and lime juice to the slow cooker insert.
4. Stir in the canned coconut milk 30 minutes before serving. Let the cooking cycle finish, then strain and serve the chicken and veggies with some of the coconut-lime sauce.
5. Prepare the salad.
6. Serve Slow Cooker Coconut Lime Chicken with garnishes and side salad.

Prepare to Freeze Directions

- Cut 4 small chicken breasts into bite-size pieces.
- Seed and finely chop 1 red bell peppers. Chop 1/2 red onion.
- To gallon-size plastic freezer baggie, add the following ingredients:
  - Chicken breast pieces
  - Chopped red bell peppers
  - Chopped red onion
  - 1 cup chicken stock
  - 2 Tbsp lime juice
  - Do NOT add coconut milk to freezer bag.
- Remove as much air as possible and seal. Add label to baggie and freeze.

Freeze & Thaw Directions

Put baggie in the freezer and freeze up to 6 months in fridge freezer or 12 months in a deep freezer. Thaw in the fridge overnight, or a warm bowl of water for about 20 minutes. Transfer all of the content from the freezer bag to slow cooker, add the canned coconut milk, and cook as directed.

Slow Cooker Cuban Chicken

Yield: 4 servings
Prep Time: 10 minutes
Cook Time: 8 hours in slow cooker

Ingredients

- 4 small boneless, skinless chicken breasts
- Salt and pepper
- 1/4 cup orange juice
- 3 Tbsp lime juice
- 2 tsp minced garlic
- 2 tsp paprika
- 1 tsp dried oregano
- 1 tsp onion powder
- 1 tsp ground cumin
- Side: cauliflower rice
- Side: veggies
- 1 gallon-size freezer baggie

Cooking Directions

1. In a small mixing bowl, whisk together the orange juice, lime juice, minced garlic, paprika, dried oregano, onion powder and ground cumin.
2. Place the chicken breasts into the base of the slow cooker and add pour the sauce over the top.
3. Set on low and cook for 8 hours. Once done cooking, shred the chicken into the sauce. Strain, if needed.
4. Cook the cauliflower rice, as directed.
5. Prepare veggies.
6. Serve Slow Cooker Cuban Chicken over cauliflower rice with veggies.

Prepare to Freeze Directions

- In a small mixing bowl, whisk together 1/4 cup orange juice, 3 Tbsp lime juice, 2 tsp minced garlic, 2 tsp paprika, 1 tsp dried oregano, 1 tsp onion powder, and 1 tsp ground cumin.
- To gallon-size plastic freezer baggie, add the following ingredients:
    - 4 boneless, skinless chicken breasts
    - Salt and pepper
    - Prepared marinade
- Remove as much air as possible and seal. Add label to baggie and freeze.

Freeze & Thaw Directions

Put baggie in the freezer and freeze up to 6 months in fridge freezer or 12 months in a deep freezer. Thaw in the fridge overnight, or a warm bowl of water for about 20 minutes, before transferring to the slow cooker and cooking on low for 8 hours.

Slow Cooker Garlic-Orange Pork Tenderloin

Yield: 4 servings
Prep Time: 5 minutes
Cook Time: 8 hours in slow cooker

Ingredients

- 2 lb. pork tenderloin
- Salt and pepper
- 1 cup orange juice
- 2 tsp minced garlic
- 1 tsp ground ginger
- 1 tsp dried thyme
- Side: mashed sweet potatoes
- Side: veggies
- 1 gallon-size freezer baggie

Cooking Directions

1. Place the pork tenderloin into the base of the slow cooker and season with salt and pepper. Pour the orange juice on and around the pork and then add the minced garlic, ground ginger and dried thyme over the top.
2. Set the slow cooker on low and cook for 8 hours. Remove from slow cooker and let rest for 5 to 10 minutes before slicing.
3. Prepare the mashed sweet potatoes.
4. Prepare veggies.
5. Serve Slow Cooker Garlic-Orange Pork Tenderloin with mashed sweet potatoes and veggies.

Prepare to Freeze Directions

- To gallon-size plastic freezer baggie, add the following ingredients:
  - 2 lb. pork tenderloin
  - Salt and pepper
  - 1 cup orange juice
  - 2 tsp minced garlic
  - 1 tsp ground ginger
  - 1 tsp dried thyme
- Remove as much air as possible and seal. Add label to baggie and freeze.

Freeze & Thaw Directions

Put baggie in the freezer and freeze up to 6 months in fridge freezer or 12 months in a deep freezer. Thaw in the fridge overnight, or a warm bowl of water for about 20 minutes, before transferring to the slow cooker and cooking on low for 8 hours.

Slow Cooker Green Chile Chicken

Yield: 4 servings
Prep Time: 10 minutes
Cook Time: 8 hours in slow cooker

Ingredients

- 8 boneless, skinless chicken thighs
- 1/4 cup lime juice
- 2 tsp ground cumin
- 1 tsp garlic powder
- 4 tomatillos
- 1/2 small white onion
- 4 oz. can green chiles
- Salt and pepper
- Garnish: lime wedges and cilantro
- Side: cauliflower rice
- Side: veggies
- 1 gallon-size freezer baggie

Cooking Directions

1. Peel off the husk and cut the tomatillos into quarters. Dice white onion.
2. Place the chicken thighs into the base of the slow cooker and add the lime juice, ground cumin, garlic powder, quartered tomatillos, diced onion and green chiles on top of the chicken. Season with salt and pepper.
3. Set the slow cooker on low and cook for 8 hours.
4. Cook the cauliflower rice, as directed.
5. Once finished cooking, shred the chicken with 2 forks and mix into the sauce. Spoon the shredded chicken over the cauliflower rice.
6. Prepare veggies and garnish.
7. Serve Slow Cooker Green Chile Chicken over cauliflower rice, garnished with lime wedges and cilantro with a side of veggies.

Prepare to Freeze Directions

- Peel off the husk and cut 4 tomatillos into quarters.
- Dice 1/2 small white onion.
- Open the can of green chiles.
- To gallon-size plastic freezer baggie, add the following ingredients:
  - 8 boneless, skinless chicken thighs
  - 1/4 cup lime juice
  - 2 tsp ground cumin
  - 1 tsp garlic powder
  - Quartered tomatillos
  - Diced onions
  - Canned green chilies
  - Salt and pepper
- Remove as much air as possible and seal. Add label to baggie and freeze.

Freeze & Thaw Directions

Put baggie in the freezer and freeze up to 6 months in fridge freezer or 12 months in a deep freezer. Thaw in the fridge overnight, or a warm bowl of water for about 20 minutes, before transferring to the slow cooker and cooking on low for 8 hours.

Slow Cooker Mango Chicken

Yield: 4 servings
Prep Time: 10 minutes
Cook Time: 8 hours in slow cooker

Ingredients

- 6 boneless, skinless chicken thighs
- 1 tsp olive oil
- 2 tsp red wine vinegar
- 1 tsp garlic powder
- Salt and pepper
- 1 small red onion
- 1 medium zucchini
- 1 mango
- 15 oz. can diced tomatoes
- Side: riced broccoli
- 1 gallon-size freezer baggie

Cooking Directions

1. Dice the red onion and mango into 1/2-inch pieces, and slice the zucchini into 1/2-inch circles.
2. Place the chicken thighs into the base of the slow cooker. Drizzle the olive oil and vinegar over the top of the chicken. Season the chicken with garlic powder, salt and pepper.
3. Place the diced red onion, zucchini slices, mango pieces, and drained diced tomatoes over top and around the chicken thighs.
4. Set slow cooker on low and cook for 8 hours. Strain chicken, veggies and fruit. Shred chicken, if desired.
5. Cook the rice broccoli as directed.
6. Serve Slow Cooker Mango Chicken with riced broccoli.

Prepare to Freeze Directions

- Dice 1 red onion. Slice 1 medium zucchini. Dice 1 mango.
- Open and drain 1 can of diced tomatoes.
- To gallon-size plastic freezer baggie, add the following ingredients:
  - 6 boneless, skinless chicken thighs
  - 1 tsp olive oil
  - 2 tsp red wine vinegar
  - 1 tsp garlic powder
  - Salt and pepper
  - Diced red onion
  - Thinly sliced zucchini
  - Seeded and diced mango
  - Canned diced tomatoes
- Remove as much air as possible and seal. Add label to baggie and freeze.

Freeze & Thaw Directions

Put baggie in the freezer and freeze up to 6 months in fridge freezer or 12 months in a deep freezer. Thaw in the fridge overnight, or a warm bowl of water for about 20 minutes, before transferring to the slow cooker and cooking on low for 8 hours.

Slow Cooker Margarita Chicken

Yield: 4 servings
Prep Time: 10 minutes
Cook Time: 8 hours in slow cooker

Ingredients

- 4 small boneless, skinless chicken breasts
- 1 cup lime juice
- 3 Tbsp honey or compliant sweetener
- 1/2 cup orange juice
- 4 tsp minced garlic
- 1/4 tsp cayenne pepper
- Salt and pepper
- Garnish: chopped cilantro
- Side: cauliflower rice
- Side: veggies
- 1 gallon-size freezer baggie

Cooking Directions

1. In a small mixing bowl, whisk together the lime juice, honey or compliant sweetener, orange juice, minced garlic, cayenne pepper and a few pinches of salt and pepper.
2. Place the chicken breasts in the base of the slow cooker and pour the marinade over the top.
3. Set on low and cook for 8 hours. Once cooked, remove from the sauce and slice or shred the chicken.
4. Cook the cauliflower rice, as directed.
5. Prepare veggies.
6. Serve Slow Cooker Margarita Chicken with chopped cilantro garnish over cauliflower rice with veggies.

Prepare to Freeze Directions

- To gallon-size plastic freezer baggie, add the following ingredients:
  - 4 small boneless, skinless chicken breasts
  - 1 cup lime juice
  - 3 Tbsp honey or compliant sweetener
  - 1/2 cup orange juice
  - 4 tsp minced garlic
  - 1/4 tsp cayenne pepper
  - Salt and pepper
- Remove as much air as possible and seal. Add label to baggie and freeze.

Freeze & Thaw Directions

Put baggie in the freezer and freeze up to 6 months in fridge freezer or 12 months in a deep freezer. Thaw in the fridge overnight, or a warm bowl of water for about 20 minutes, before transferring to the slow cooker and cooking on low for 8 hours.

New Mexican Chicken Lettuce Wraps {Filling}

Yield: 4 servings
Prep Time: 10 minutes
Cook Time: 8 hours in slow cooker

(K) (P) (W30)

Ingredients

- 4 small boneless, skinless chicken breasts
- 1 cup red salsa
- 4 oz. can green chiles
- 1 Tbsp minced onion
- 1 Tbsp ground cumin
- 1 tsp garlic powder
- Salt and pepper
- Garnish: chopped cilantro
- Side: lettuce leaves
- Side: veggies
- 1 gallon-size freezer baggie

Cooking Directions

1. Place the chicken breasts into the base of the slow cooker and add the red salsa, green chiles, minced onion, ground cumin, garlic powder and salt and pepper.
2. Set the slow cooker on low and cook for 8 hours. Once finished cooking, shred the chicken with 2 forks and mix into the sauce.
3. Spoon the shredded chicken into lettuce leaves and make lettuce wraps.
4. Prepare veggies.
5. Slow Cooker New Mexican Chicken Lettuce Wraps with veggies.

Prepare to Freeze Directions

- To gallon-size plastic freezer baggie, add the following ingredients:
  - 4 small boneless, skinless chicken breasts
  - 1 cup red salsa
  - 4 oz. can green chiles
  - 1 Tbsp minced onion
  - 1 Tbsp ground cumin
  - 1 tsp garlic powder
  - Salt and pepper
- Remove as much air as possible and seal. Add label to baggie and freeze.

Freeze & Thaw Directions

Put baggie in the freezer and freeze up to 6 months in fridge freezer or 12 months in a deep freezer. Thaw in the fridge overnight, or a warm bowl of water for about 20 minutes, before transferring to a slow cooker and cooking as directed.

Slow Cooker Pineapple & Salsa Verde Chicken

Yield: 4 servings
Prep Time: 10 minutes
Cook Time: 8 hours in slow cooker

Ingredients

- 4 small boneless, skinless chicken breasts
- 1 cup salsa verde sauce
- 8 oz. can crushed pineapple
- 1 Tbsp minced onion
- 1 tsp minced garlic
- Salt and pepper
- Garnish: jalapeños
- Garnish: chopped cilantro
- Side: veggies
- Side: salad
- 1 gallon-size freezer baggie

Cooking Directions

1. Open the can of crushed pineapple.
2. Place the chicken breasts in the base of the slow cooker and pour the salsa verde and crushed pineapple over and around the chicken. Sprinkle in the minced onion and minced garlic. Season with salt and pepper.
3. Set on low and cook for 8 hours. Once cooked, shred the chicken with 2 forks. Strain and serve.
4. Prepare veggies.
5. Prepare the salad.
6. Serve Slow Cooker Pineapple & Salsa Verde Chicken with chopped jalapeno and chopped cilantro garnish, with veggies and side salad.

Prepare to Freeze Directions

- Open the can of crushed pineapple.
- To gallon-size plastic freezer baggie, add the following ingredients:
  - 4 small boneless, skinless chicken breasts
  - 1 cup salsa verde
  - 8 oz. can crushed pineapple
  - 1 Tbsp minced onion
  - 1 tsp minced garlic
  - Salt and pepper
- Remove as much air as possible and seal. Add label to baggie and freeze.

Freeze & Thaw Directions

Put baggie in the freezer and freeze up to 6 months in fridge freezer or 12 months in a deep freezer. Thaw in the fridge overnight, or a warm bowl of water for about 20 minutes, before transferring to the slow cooker and cooking on low for 8 hours. Shred the chicken and strain before serving.

Slow Cooker Ranchero Chicken

Yield:	4 servings
Prep Time:	10 minutes
Cook Time:	8 hours in slow cooker

Ingredients

- 2 boneless, skinless chicken breasts
- 4 boneless, skinless chicken thighs
- 15 oz. can diced tomatoes
- 6 oz. can tomato paste
- 3 Tbsp taco seasoning (homemade recipe below)
- Salt and pepper
- Side: cauliflower rice
- Side: veggies
- 1 gallon-size freezer baggie

Cooking Directions

1. Whisk together the diced tomatoes with their juices and the tomato paste in the base of the slow cooker. Stir in the taco seasoning.
2. Add the chicken breast and thighs to sauce and spoon the sauce over the top. Set the slow cooker on low and cook for 8 hours.
3. Once cooked, pull apart the chicken with 2 forks. This shredded chicken-tomato mixture could also be used for enchiladas, on tostadas, in burritos or hard shell tacos. Also, the extra cooked and shredded chicken can be cooled and frozen to use again in the future.
4. Cook the cauliflower rice, as directed.
5. Prepare veggies.
6. Serve Ranchero Chicken over cauliflower rice with side of veggies.

Prepare to Freeze Directions

- Open the can of diced tomatoes.
- Open the can of tomato paste.
- To gallon-size plastic freezer baggie, add the following ingredients:
  - Can of diced tomatoes
  - Can of tomato paste
  - 3 Tbsp taco seasoning
  - 2 boneless, skinless chicken breasts
  - 4 boneless chicken thighs
  - Salt and pepper
- Remove as much air as possible and seal. Add label to baggie and freeze.

Freeze & Thaw Directions

Put baggie in the freezer and freeze up to 6 months in fridge freezer or 12 months in a deep freezer. Thaw in the fridge overnight, or a warm bowl of water for about 20 minutes, before transferring to the slow cooker and cooking on low for 8 hours.

Special Note: *Homemade taco seasoning mix recipe is here - www.5dollardinners.com/ homemade-taco-seasoning.*

Slow Cooker Ropa Vieja

Yield: 4 servings
Prep Time: 10 minutes
Cook Time: 8 hours in slow cooker

Ingredients

- 2 lb. flank steak or skirt steak
- Salt and pepper
- 1 red bell pepper
- 1 green bell pepper
- 1 small white onion
- 15 oz. can crushed tomatoes
- 1 Tbsp apple cider vinegar
- 1 Tbsp cumin
- 1/2 cup green olives
- Side: cauliflower rice
- Side: salad
- 1 gallon-size freezer baggie

Cooking Directions

1. Seed and slice the bell peppers. Slice the onion.
2. Place the flank steak into the base of the slow cooker and season with salt and pepper. Add the sliced bell peppers and onions, crushed tomatoes, vinegar, cumin and green olives.
3. Set the slow cooker on low and cook for 8 hours. Once finished cooking, shred the flank steak with 2 forks and mix into the sauce.
4. Cook the cauliflower rice, as directed.
5. Spoon the shredded beef over rice.
6. Prepare the salad.
7. Serve Slow Cooker Ropa Vieja over cauliflower rice with salad.

Prepare to Freeze Directions

- Seed and slice 1 green bell pepper and 1 red bell pepper.
- Slice 1 onion.
- To gallon-size plastic freezer baggie, add the following ingredients:
  - 2 lb. flank steak or skirt steak
  - Salt and pepper
  - Sliced green and red bell peppers
  - Sliced onions
  - 15 oz. can crushed tomatoes
  - 1 Tbsp apple cider vinegar
  - 1 Tbsp cumin
  - 1/2 cup green olives
- Remove as much air as possible and seal. Add label to baggie and freeze.

Freeze & Thaw Directions

Put baggie in the freezer and freeze up to 6 months in fridge freezer or 12 months in a deep freezer. Thaw in the fridge overnight, or a warm bowl of water for about 20 minutes, before transferring to the slow cooker and cooking on low for 8 hours.

Slow Cooker Santa Fe Beef

Yield: 4 servings
Prep Time: 10 minutes
Cook Time: 8 hours in slow cooker

Ingredients

- 2 lb. beef chuck roast
- Salt and pepper
- 2 Tbsp taco seasoning (homemade recipe below)
- 4 oz. can green chiles
- 1 cup red salsa
- Side: salad
- Side: cauliflower rice
- 1 gallon-size freezer baggie

Cooking Directions

1. Place the beef roast into the base of the slow cooker and season with salt and pepper. Sprinkle the taco seasoning over the roast. Pour the green chilies and red salsa over the top.
2. Set the slow cooker on low and cook for 8 hours. Once finished cooking, shred the beef with 2 forks and mix into the sauce.
3. Prepare salad.
4. Prepare the cauliflower rice.
5. Serve Slow Cooker Santa Fe Beef with salad and cauliflower rice.

Prepare to Freeze Directions

- Open the can of green chiles.
- To gallon-size plastic freezer baggie, add the following ingredients:
  - 2 lb. beef chuck roast
  - Salt and pepper
  - 2 Tbsp taco seasoning
  - 4 oz. can green chilies
  - 1 cup red salsa
- Remove as much air as possible and seal. Add label to baggie and freeze.

Freeze & Thaw Directions

Put baggie in the freezer and freeze up to 6 months in fridge freezer or 12 months in a deep freezer. Thaw in the fridge overnight, or a warm bowl of water for about 20 minutes, before transferring to the slow cooker and cooking on low for 8 hours.

Special Note: *Homemade taco seasoning mix recipe is here - www.5dollardinners.com/homemade-taco-seasoning*

Slow Cooker Southwestern Pork Roast

Yield: 4 servings
Prep Time: 10 minutes
Cook Time: 8 hours in slow cooker

Ingredients

- 2 lb. pork roast
- Salt and pepper
- 2 Tbsp honey or compliant sweetener
- 2 Tbsp minced onion
- 1 Tbsp chili powder
- 1 Tbsp ground cumin
- 2 - 4 oz. cans green chiles
- Side: zoodles
- Side: salad
- 1 gallon-size freezer baggie

Cooking Directions

1. In a small mixing bowl, combine the honey or compliant sweetener, minced onion, chili powder and ground cumin.
2. Place the pork roast in the base of the slow cooker and season with salt and pepper. Then add the spice mixture directly onto the pork. Top with cans of green chilies onto the pork roast.
3. Set the slow cooker on low and cook for 8 hours.
4. Please note: if your slow cooker "runs hot," you might want to add 1/2 to 3/4 cup of water to keep the roast from drying out.
5. Cook the zoodles, as directed.
6. Prepare the salad.
7. Serve Slow Cooker Southwestern Pork Roast with zoodles and salad.

Prepare to Freeze Directions

- In a small mixing bowl, combine 2 Tbsp honey or compliant sweetener, 2 Tbsp minced onion, 1 Tbsp chili powder and 1 Tbsp ground cumin.
- Open 2 cans of green chilies.
- To gallon-size plastic freezer baggie, add the following ingredients:
  ○ 2 lb. pork roast
  ○ Salt and pepper
  ○ Spice mixture
  ○ Canned green chilies
- Remove as much air as possible and seal. Add label to baggie and freeze.

Freeze & Thaw Directions

Put baggie in the freezer and freeze up to 6 months in fridge freezer or 12 months in a deep freezer. Thaw in the fridge overnight, or a warm bowl of water for about 20 minutes, before transferring to the slow cooker and cooking on low for 8 hours.

Slow Cooker Spinach Artichoke Chicken

Yield: 4 servings
Prep Time: 10 minutes
Cook Time: 8 hours in slow cooker

Ingredients

- 4 small boneless, skinless chicken breasts
- 1 tsp garlic powder
- Salt and pepper
- 1 cup Parmesan cheese
- 2 cups shredded mozzarella cheese
- 10 oz. box frozen spinach
- 15 oz. can artichoke hearts
- 8 oz. cream cheese
- Side: salad
- 1 gallon-size freezer baggie

Cooking Directions

1. Warm and drain the spinach. Cut the cream cheese into small cubes.
2. Open and drain the quartered artichoke hearts.
3. Place the chicken breasts into the base of the slow cooker and season with garlic powder, salt and pepper.
4. In a small mixing bowl, combine the Parmesan cheese, mozzarella cheese, drained spinach, cream cheese cubes, and quartered artichokes. Spread the cheesy mixture over the chicken in the slow cooker.
5. Set the slow cooker on low and cook for 8 hours.
6. Prepare the salad.
7. Serve Slow Cooker Spinach Artichoke Chicken with side salad.

Prepare to Freeze Directions

- Warm and drain 10 oz. of spinach.
- Cut up 8 oz. block cream cheese into small cubes.
- Open and drain 1 can of quartered artichoke hearts.
- In a small mixing bowl, combine 1 cups Parmesan cheese, 2 cups mozzarella cheese, the drained spinach, the cream cheese cubes, and the quartered artichoke hearts.
- To gallon-size plastic freezer baggie, add the following ingredients:
  ○ 4 small boneless, skinless chicken breasts
  ○ 1 tsp garlic powder
  ○ Salt and pepper
  ○ Cheesy mixture
- Remove as much air as possible and seal. Add label to baggie and freeze.

Freeze & Thaw Directions

Put baggie in the freezer and freeze up to 6 months in fridge freezer or 12 months in a deep freezer. Thaw in the fridge overnight, or a warm bowl of water for about 20 minutes, before transferring to the slow cooker and cooking on low for 8 hours.

Slow Cooker Sweet Potato & Chicken Curry

Yield: 4 servings
Prep Time: 10 minutes
Cook Time: 8 hours in slow cooker

Ingredients

- 15 oz. can light coconut milk
- 3 tsp curry powder
- 1 tsp ground ginger
- 1 tsp salt
- 8 boneless, skinless chicken thighs
- 4 medium sweet potatoes
- 8 whole carrots
- 1 small white onion
- Side: veggies
- 1 gallon-size freezer baggie

Cooking Directions

1. Peel and quarter the sweet potatoes.
2. Peel and slice the carrots.
3. Dice the onion.
4. Whisk together the coconut milk, curry powder, ground ginger and salt in the base of the slow cooker. Add the chicken thighs, sweet potatoes, carrots and onion. Set the slow cooker on low and cook for 8 hours.
5. Prepare veggies.
6. Serve Slow Cooker Sweet Potato and Chicken Curry with veggies.

Prepare to Freeze Directions

- Dice 1 white onion.
- Peel and quarter 4 sweet potatoes.
- Peel and slice 8 carrots.
- To gallon-size plastic freezer baggie, add the following ingredients:
  - 8 boneless chicken thighs
  - Sweet potatoes
  - Carrots
  - Onions
  - 3 Tbsp curry powder
  - 1 tsp ground ginger
  - 1 tsp salt
  - Do NOT freeze the coconut milk. You will add it at the time of slow cooking.
- Remove as much air as possible and seal. Add label to baggie and freeze.

Freeze & Thaw Directions

Put baggie in the freezer and freeze up to 6 months in fridge freezer or 12 months in a deep freezer. Thaw in the fridge overnight, or a warm bowl of water for about 20 minutes, before transferring to the slow cooker, stirring in the canned coconut milk, and cooking on low for 8 hours.

Chapter 4 - Stovetop Recipes

Beef & Sweet Potato Stew

Bacon Cheeseburger Chili

Beef Red Curry

Chipotle Chili

Cuban Chili

Poor Man's Paleo Stew

Paleo Minestrone Soup

Mediterranean Chicken Thighs

Mediterranean Pork Chops

Beef & Sweet Potato Stew

Yield: 4 servings
Prep Time: 10 minutes
Cook Time: 30 minutes

Ingredients

- 1 Tbsp olive oil
- 1 lb. stew beef cubes
- 4 small sweet potatoes
- 4 whole carrots
- 2 celery stalks
- 1 small white onion
- 4 cups beef broth
- 6 oz. can tomato paste
- 1 tsp paprika
- 1 tsp dried thyme
- Salt and pepper
- Side: salad
- 1 gallon-size freezer baggie

Cooking Directions

1. Open can of tomato paste.
2. Peel and dice the sweet potatoes. Peel and dice the carrots.
3. Chop the celery. Chop the onion.
4. In a large saucepan, heat the olive oil and brown the stew beef cubes. Stir in the chopped celery, onion, sweet potatoes and carrots and saute for 3 to 5 minutes, tossing often. Stir in the beef broth and tomato paste. Whisk in the paprika and dried thyme. Bring to bubbling and reduce heat and simmer for 10 minutes to allow flavors to mingle.
5. Prepare the salad.
6. Serve Beef & Sweet Potato Stew with salad.

Prepare to Freeze Directions

- Peel and dice 4 sweet potatoes. Peel and dice 4 carrots.
- Chop 2 celery stalks. Chop 1 onion.
- Open the can of tomato paste.
- To gallon-size plastic freezer baggie, add the following ingredients:
  - 1 lb. stew beef cubes
  - Diced sweet potatoes
  - Diced carrots
  - Chopped celery
  - Chopped onion
  - 4 cups beef broth
  - 6 oz. can tomato paste
  - 1 tsp paprika
  - 1 tsp dried thyme
  - Salt and pepper
- Remove as much air as possible and seal. Add label to baggie and freeze.

Freeze & Thaw Directions

Put baggie in the freezer and freeze up to 6 months in fridge freezer or 12 months in a deep freezer. Thaw in the fridge overnight, or a bowl of warm water for about 20 minutes, before transferring to a saucepan and cooking. Bring to boil and then reduce heat and simmer for 10 minutes.

Bacon Cheeseburger Chili

Yield:	4 servings
Prep Time:	15 minutes
Cook Time:	30 minutes

Ingredients

- 1 lb. ground beef
- 1 Tbsp minced onion
- 1 tsp garlic powder
- 2 cups beef broth
- 1 cup shredded cheddar cheese
- 2 cups heavy cream
- Salt and pepper
- Garnish: crumbled strips bacon
- Side: veggies
- 1 gallon-size freezer baggie

Cooking Directions

1. In a large saucepan, brown the ground beef with the minced onion and garlic powder. Drain and return to saucepan. Stir in the beef broth. Bring to bubbling and reduce heat and simmer for 5 minutes to allow flavors to mingle.
2. Stir in the cream and HALF of the shredded cheese to the chili and simmer for 10 minutes. Use remaining shredded cheese for garnish. Season with salt and pepper to taste.
3. Cook and crumble the bacon, if needed.
4. Prepare veggies.
5. Serve Bacon Cheeseburger Chili with bacon and shredded cheese garnish, and side of veggies.

Prepare to Freeze Directions

- Brown 1 lb. ground beef with 1 Tbsp minced onion and 1 tsp garlic powder. Set aside to cool.
- To gallon-size plastic freezer baggie, add the following ingredients:
  - Browned ground beef
  - 2 cups beef broth
  - Salt and pepper
- Do not add cream or cheese to freezer meal bag.
- Remove as much air as possible and seal. Add label to baggie and freeze.

Freeze & Thaw Directions

Put baggie in the freezer and freeze up to 6 months in fridge freezer or 12 months in a deep freezer. Thaw in the fridge overnight, or a warm bowl of water for about 20 minutes, before transferring to a saucepan and reheating. Stir in heavy cream and half of the shredded cheese about 10 minutes before serving. Use remaining cheese for garnish in each bowl, and top with crumbled bacon.

Beef Red Curry

Yield: 4 servings
Prep Time: 15 minutes
Cook Time: 15 minutes

Ingredients

- 2 - 15 oz. cans coconut milk
- 3 Tbsp red curry paste
- 1 Tbsp curry powder
- 1 tsp ground ginger
- 1 tsp garlic powder
- 1 red bell pepper
- 12 oz. bag matchstick carrots
- 1 lb. beef strips for stirfry
- Garnish: cilantro and green onion
- Side: cauliflower rice
- 1 gallon-size freezer baggie

Cooking Directions

1. Cook the cauliflower rice, as directed.
2. In a large saucepan or skillet, whisk the coconut milk, curry paste, curry powder, ginger and garlic powder. If your coconut milk has separated in the can, it will become smooth again when it heats up.
3. Stir in the bell pepper slices, shredded carrots and beef strips. Let cook for about 15 minutes, allowing the beef to cook through, the veggies to soften and the flavors to mingle.
4. Serve Beef Red Curry over cauliflower rice with optional cilantro and green onion garnish.

Prepare to Freeze Directions

- Slice 1 red bell pepper.
- Whisk together 2 - 15 oz. cans coconut milk, 3 Tbsp red curry paste, 1 Tbsp curry powder, 1 tsp ground ginger, and 1 tsp garlic powder.
- To gallon-size plastic freezer baggie, add the following ingredients:
  - Sliced bell peppers
  - 12 oz. matchstick carrots
  - 1 lb. beef strips for stirfry
  - Prepared sauce
- Remove as much air as possible and seal. Add label to baggie and freeze.

Freeze & Thaw Directions

Put baggie in the freezer and freeze up to 6 months in fridge freezer or 12 months in a deep freezer. Thaw in the fridge overnight, or a warm bowl of water for about 20 minutes before cooking in skillet or saucepan.

Chipotle Chili

Yield: 4 servings
Prep Time: 15 minutes
Cook Time: 30 minutes

Ingredients

- 1 lb. ground beef
- 1 Tbsp minced onion
- 1 tsp garlic powder
- 1 red bell pepper
- 15 oz. can tomato sauce
- 1 Tbsp chili powder
- 1 tsp chipotle chili powder
- 1 tsp ground cumin
- 2 cups beef broth
- Salt and pepper
- Side: salad
- 1 gallon-size freezer baggie

Cooking Directions

1. Open and drain the can of tomato sauce.
2. Seed and chop the red bell pepper.
3. In a large saucepan, brown the ground beef with the minced onion and garlic powder. Drain and return to saucepan. Stir in the chopped red bell pepper, tomato sauce, chili powder, chipotle chili powder, ground cumin and saute for 5 minutes.
4. Stir in the beef broth and let simmer for 10 minutes to allow the flavors to mingle. Season with salt and pepper to taste.
5. Prepare the salad.
6. Serve Chipotle Chili with salad.

Prepare to Freeze Directions

- Brown 1 lb. ground beef with 1 Tbsp minced onion and 1 tsp garlic powder. Let cool.
- Seed and chop 1 red bell peppers.
- Open and drain 1 can of tomato sauce.
- To gallon-size plastic freezer baggie, add the following ingredients:
  - Browned ground beef
  - 15 oz. can tomato sauce
  - Chopped bell peppers
  - 1 Tbsp chili powder
  - 1 tsp chipotle chili powder
  - 1 tsp ground cumin
  - 2 cups beef broth
  - Salt and pepper
- Remove as much air as possible and seal. Add label to baggie and freeze.

Freeze & Thaw Directions

Put baggie in the freezer and freeze up to 6 months in fridge freezer or 12 months in a deep freezer. Thaw in the fridge overnight, or a warm bowl of water for about 20 minutes, before transferring all of the contents of the baggie into large saucepan or Dutch oven. Bring to bubbling and cook for 20 minutes.

Cuban Chili

Yield:	4 servings
Prep Time:	15 minutes
Cook Time:	30 minutes

Ingredients

- 1 lb. ground beef
- 1 Tbsp minced onion
- 1 tsp garlic powder
- 1 green bell pepper
- 15 oz. can diced tomatoes
- 1 Tbsp chili powder
- 1 tsp ground cumin
- 1 tsp dried oregano
- 1/2 tsp cinnamon
- 2 cups beef broth
- 1 cup unsweetened raisins
- Salt and pepper
- Side: salad
- 1 gallon-size freezer baggie

Cooking Directions

1. Open and drain the can of diced tomatoes.
2. Seed and chop the green bell pepper.
3. In a large saucepan, brown the ground beef with the minced onion and garlic powder. Drain and return to saucepan. Stir in the chopped bell pepper, diced tomatoes, chili powder, ground cumin, dried oregano, and cinnamon and saute for 5 minutes.
4. Stir in the beef broth and unsweetened raisins and let simmer for 10 minutes to allow the flavors to mingle. Season with salt and pepper to taste.
5. Prepare the salad.
6. Serve Cuban Chili with salad.

Prepare to Freeze Directions

- Brown 1 lb. ground beef with 1 Tbsp minced onion and 1 tsp garlic powder. Let cool.
- Seed and chop 1 green bell pepper.
- Open and drain 1 can of diced tomatoes.
- To gallon-size plastic freezer baggie, add the following ingredients:
  - Browned ground beef
  - Diced tomatoes
  - Chopped bell peppers
  - 1 Tbsp chili powder
  - 1 tsp ground cumin
  - 1 tsp dried oregano
  - 1/2 tsp cinnamon
  - 2 cups beef broth
  - 1 cup unsweetened raisins
  - Salt and pepper
- Remove as much air as possible and seal. Add label to baggie and freeze.

Freeze & Thaw Directions

Put baggie in the freezer and freeze up to 6 months in fridge freezer or 12 months in a deep freezer. Thaw in the fridge overnight, or a warm bowl of water for about 20 minutes, before transferring all of the contents of the baggie into large saucepan or Dutch oven. Bring to bubbling and cook for 20 minutes.

Special Note: *Omit the unsweetened raisins for complete keto meal.*

Poor Man's Paleo Soup

Yield: 4 servings
Prep Time: 15 minutes
Cook Time: 25 minutes

Ingredients

- 1 lb. ground beef
- 4 small sweet potatoes
- 4 whole carrots
- 1 small white onion
- 4 cups beef broth
- 6 oz. can tomato paste
- 1 tsp paprika
- 1 tsp dried thyme
- Salt and pepper
- Side: salad
- 1 gallon-size freezer baggie

Cooking Directions

1. Open can of tomato paste.
2. Peel and dice the sweet potatoes. Peel and dice the carrots.
3. Chop the onion.
4. In a large saucepan, brown the ground beef. Drain, if needed, and return to saucepan.
5. Stir in the diced onion, sweet potatoes and carrots and saute for 3 to 5 minutes, tossing often. Stir in the beef broth and tomato paste. Whisk in the paprika and dried thyme. Bring to bubbling and reduce heat and simmer for 10 minutes to allow flavors to mingle. Season with salt and pepper, as needed.
6. Prepare the salad.
7. Serve Poor Man's Paleo Soup with salad.

Prepare to Freeze Directions

- Brown 1 lb. ground beef. Drain and set aside to cool.
- Peel and dice 4 sweet potatoes. Peel and dice 4 carrots.
- Chop 1 white onion.
- Open the cans of tomato paste.
- To gallon-size plastic freezer baggie in a round bowl/dish, add the following ingredients:
  - Browned ground beef
  - Diced sweet potatoes
  - Diced carrots
  - Chopped onion
  - 4 cups beef broth
  - 6 oz. can tomato paste
  - 1 tsp paprika
  - 1 tsp dried thyme
  - Salt and pepper
- Remove as much air as possible and seal. Add label to baggie and freeze.

Freeze & Thaw Directions

Put baggie in the freezer and freeze up to 6 months in fridge freezer or 12 months in a deep freezer. Thaw in the fridge overnight, or a bowl of warm water for about 20 minutes, before transferring to a saucepan and cooking. Bring to boil and then reduce heat and simmer for 10 minutes.

Paleo Minestrone Soup

Yield: 4 servings
Prep Time: 20 minutes
Cook Time: 30 minutes

Ingredients

- 2 Tbsp olive oil
- 1 small white onion
- 2 celery stalks
- 2 garlic cloves
- 4 whole carrots
- 1/2 lb. green beans
- 2 medium zucchini
- 1 cup cauliflower rice
- 15 oz. can tomato sauce
- 1 Tbsp Italian seasoning
- 6 cups chicken or vegetable stock
- Salt and pepper
- Side: salad
- 1 gallon-size freezer baggie

Cooking Directions

1. In a large saucepan, heat the olive oil and saute the onion, celery, garlic and carrots for 4 to 5 minutes. Stir in the green beans, zucchini, cauliflower rice, tomato sauce, Italian seasoning and chicken stock. Bring to bubbling.
2. Remove soup from the heat and prepare to spoon into serving bowls.
3. Serve Paleo Minestrone Soup with and side salad.

Prepare to Freeze Directions

- Chop 1 white onion.
- Peel and chop 4 whole carrots.
- Slice 2 celery stalks.
- Trim 1/2 lb. green beans.
- Thinly slice 2 medium zucchini.
- Open the can of tomato sauce.
- To gallon-size plastic freezer baggie, add the following ingredients:
  ○ Chopped onion
  ○ Chopped celery
  ○ 2 garlic cloves, crushed
  ○ Chopped carrots
  ○ Trimmed green beans
  ○ Sliced zucchini
  ○ 1 cup riced cauliflower
  ○ 15 oz. can tomato sauce
  ○ 1 Tbsp Italian seasoning blend
  ○ 6 cups chicken or vegetable stock
- Remove as much air as possible and seal. Add label to baggie and freeze.

Freeze & Thaw Directions

Put baggie in the freezer and freeze up to 6 months in fridge freezer or 12 months in a deep freezer. Thaw in a warm bowl of water for about 20 minutes, before transferring all the ingredients to a large saucepan or stockpot. Reheat the soup and simmer until warmed through.

Mediterranean Chicken Thighs

Yield: 4 servings
Prep Time: 10 minutes
Cook Time: 25 minutes

Ingredients

- 2 lbs. bone-in chicken thighs
- 2 Tbsp olive oil
- 2 Tbsp balsamic vinegar
- 15 oz. can diced tomatoes
- 1/2 small red onion
- 1 cup kalamata olives
- 1 Tbsp dried oregano
- Salt and pepper
- Side: zoodles
- Side: veggies
- 1 gallon-size freezer baggie

Cooking Directions

1. Open the can of diced tomatoes.
2. Dice the red onion.
3. In a Dutch oven, add the olive oil and balsamic vinegar and brown both sides of the chicken thighs. Stir in the diced tomatoes with their juices. Add the diced red onion and kalamata olives into the tomato sauce. Sprinkle in the oregano and salt and pepper to taste. Reduce heat to medium and cook for 15 minutes, or until chicken is cooked through.
4. Cook the zoodles, as directed.
5. Prepare the veggies.
6. Serve Mediterranean Chicken Thighs over zoodles with veggies.

Prepare to Freeze Directions

- Dice 1/2 small red onion.
- Open the can of diced tomatoes.
- To gallon-size plastic freezer baggie, add the following ingredients:
  - 2 lbs. bone-in chicken thighs
  - 2 Tbsp olive oil
  - 2 Tbsp balsamic vinegar
  - Diced tomatoes
  - Diced red onion
  - 1 cup kalamata olives
  - 1 Tbsp dried oregano
  - Salt and pepper
- Remove as much air as you can and seal. Freeze up to 6 months in your fridge freezer or 12 months in a deep freezer.

Freeze & Thaw Directions

Put baggie in the freezer and freeze up to 6 months in fridge freezer or 12 months in a deep freezer. Thaw in the fridge overnight, or a warm bowl of water for about 20 minutes, before transferring to a Dutch oven and cooking the chicken and sauce over medium heat for 15 to 20 minutes, or until chicken is cooked through.

Mediterranean Pork Chops

Yield: 4 servings
Prep Time: 10 minutes
Cook Time: 25 minutes

Ingredients

- 4 small boneless pork chops
- 2 Tbsp olive oil
- 2 Tbsp balsamic vinegar
- 15 oz. can diced tomatoes
- 1/2 small red onion
- 1 cup kalamata olives
- 1 Tbsp dried oregano
- Salt and pepper
- Side: riced broccoli
- Side: veggies
- 1 gallon-size freezer baggie

Cooking Directions

1. Open the diced tomatoes.
2. Dice the red onion.
3. In a Dutch oven, add the olive oil and balsamic vinegar and brown both sides of the pork chops. Stir in the diced tomatoes with their juices. Add the diced red onion and kalamata olives into the tomato sauce. Sprinkle in the oregano and salt and pepper to taste. Reduce heat to medium and cook for 15 minutes, or until pork chops are cooked through.
4. Cook the riced broccoli, as directed.
5. Prepare the veggies.
6. Serve Mediterranean Pork Chops over riced broccoli with veggies.

Prepare to Freeze Directions

- Dice 1/2 small red onion.
- Open the can of diced tomatoes.
- To gallon-size plastic freezer baggie, add the following ingredients:
  - 4 boneless pork chops
  - 2 Tbsp olive oil
  - 2 Tbsp balsamic vinegar
  - Diced tomatoes
  - Diced red onion
  - 1 cup kalamata olives
  - 1 Tbsp dried oregano
  - Salt and pepper
- Remove as much air as you can and seal. Freeze up to 6 months in your fridge freezer or 12 months in a deep freezer.

Freeze & Thaw Directions

Put baggie in the freezer and freeze up to 6 months in fridge freezer or 12 months in a deep freezer. Thaw in the fridge overnight, or a warm bowl of water for about 20 minutes, before transferring to a Dutch oven and cooking the pork chops and sauce over medium heat for 15 to 20 minutes, or until pork chops are cooked through.

Chapter 5 - Skillet Recipes

Skillet Pork Chops with Mushrooms and Pearled Onions

Yield: 4 servings
Prep Time: 10 minutes
Cook Time: 25 minutes

Ingredients

- 4 boneless pork chops
- Salt and pepper
- 2 Tbsp olive oil
- 8 oz. baby bella mushrooms
- 10 oz. bag frozen pearled onions
- 1 tsp dried thyme
- 1 tsp dried basil
- Side: salad
- Side: zoodles
- 1 gallon-size freezer baggie

Cooking Directions

1. Heat the olive oil in skillet and saute the baby bella mushrooms and frozen pearled onions for 4 to 5 minutes. Pour them out into a bowl and set aside.
2. In the same skillet, brown the pork chops for 2 minutes on each side. Add the sauteed mushrooms and pearled onions back into the skillet and add the dried thyme and basil. Stir to combine, reduce heat and simmer for 5 to 8 minutes, or until pork chops are cooked through.
3. Prepare the salad.
4. Cook the zoodles, as directed.
5. Serve Skillet Pork Chops with Mushrooms and Pearled Onions with salad and zoodles.

Prepare to Freeze Directions

- To gallon-size plastic freezer baggie, add the following ingredients:
  - 4 boneless pork chops
  - Salt and pepper
  - 2 Tbsp olive oil
  - 8 oz. baby bella sliced mushrooms
  - 10 oz. bag frozen pearled onions
  - 1 tsp dried thyme
  - 1 tsp dried basil
- Remove as much air as possible and seal. Add label to baggie and freeze.

Freeze & Thaw Directions

Put baggie in the freezer and freeze up to 6 months in fridge freezer or 12 months in a deep freezer. Thaw in the fridge overnight, or a warm bowl of water for about 20 minutes, before transferring the veggies to a skillet and sauteing as directed. Remove veggies from pan. Then brown the pork chops on both sides, add the veggies back into the pan, and saute until the pork chops are cooked through.

Coconut Curried Salmon

Yield: 4 servings
Prep Time: 15 minutes
Cook Time: 10 minutes

Ingredients

- 1 lb. salmon
- Salt and pepper
- 2 Tbsp red curry paste
- 1 Tbsp olive oil
- 15 oz. can light coconut milk
- 1/2 tsp ground ginger
- 1/2 tsp crushed red pepper
- Side: cauliflower rice
- Side: veggies
- 1 gallon-size freezer baggie

Cooking Directions

1. Cook the cauliflower rice, as directed.
2. Season the salmon fillets with salt and pepper. Spread about 1-2 tsp of red curry paste onto the top side of each fillet.
3. Add the olive oil to a skillet, heat it up and roll it around to coat the bottom of the skillet. Place the salmon fillet 'red curry side down' into the oil and saute them for 3-4 minutes. Flip them over and then quickly pour in the coconut milk. Gently stir the coconut milk in and around the salmon, lifting the salmon so the coconut milk spreads under each of the fillets. Whisk in the ground ginger and crushed red pepper to the curry sauce.
4. Cook salmon for another 5-7 minutes, or until cooked through. Cooking time may vary depending on thickness of the fillets. Season curry sauce with salt and pepper to taste.
5. Serve Coconut Curried Salmon with rice and veggies.

Prepare to Freeze Directions

- Cut 1 lb. salmon into 4 - 1/4 lb. fillets & remove skin.
- To gallon-size plastic freezer baggie, add the following ingredients:
  - 1 lb. salmon, cut into 1/4 lb pieces, skin removed
  - Salt and pepper
  - 2 Tbsp red curry paste, evenly divided onto each piece of salmon
- Note: Do NOT add the canned coconut milk or spices at this time.
- Remove as much air as possible and seal. Add label to baggie and freeze.

Freeze & Thaw Directions

Put baggie in the freezer and freeze up to 6 months in fridge freezer or 12 months in a deep freezer. Thaw completely in the fridge overnight, or a warm bowl of water for about 20 minutes, before transferring to the skillet and cooking with canned coconut milk and spices, as directed.

Bolognese Sauce

Yield: 4 servings
Prep Time: 10 minutes
Cook Time: 25 minutes

Ingredients

- 4 slices bacon
- 1 lb. ground beef
- 1 Tbsp minced onion
- 1 tsp garlic powder
- 28 oz. can crushed tomatoes
- 1 Tbsp Italian seasoning
- 1 celery stalk
- 1/2 small white onion
- 4 cups spiralized zucchini
- Garnish: grated Parmesan cheese
- Side: veggies
- 1 gallon-size freezer baggie

Cooking Directions

1. Cook and crumble the bacon.
2. Shred the carrots. Finely chop the celery and onion.
3. In a large saucepan, brown the ground beef with the minced onion and garlic powder. Drain and return to saucepan. Stir in the crushed tomatoes, Italian seasoning, shredded carrots, chopped celery, chopped onion and crumbled bacon. Bring to bubbling and reduce heat and simmer for 5 minutes to allow flavors to mingle.
4. Prepare and cook the spiralized zucchini, as needed.
5. Prepare veggies.
6. Serve Bolognese Sauce over spiralized zucchini with grated Parmesan garnish and side of veggies.

Prepare to Freeze Directions

- Cook and crumble 4 slices bacon.
- Brown 1 lb. ground beef with 1 Tbsp minced onion and 1 tsp garlic powder. Let cool.
- To gallon-size plastic freezer baggie, add the following ingredients:
  - Browned ground beef
  - 28 oz. can crushed tomatoes
  - 1 Tbsp Italian seasoning
  - Chopped celery
  - Chopped onion
  - Cooked and crumbled bacon
- Remove as much air as you can and seal. Freeze up to 6 months in your fridge freezer or 12 months in a deep freezer.

Freeze & Thaw Directions

Put baggie in the freezer and freeze up to 6 months in fridge freezer or 12 months in a deep freezer. Thaw in the fridge overnight, or a warm bowl of water for about 20 minutes, before transferring to a saucepan and reheating.

Special Note: *Omit the grated Parmesan cheese if making Paleo or Whole30 meal.*

Peach & Balsamic Chicken Skillet

Yield: 4 servings
Prep Time: 10 minutes
Cook Time: 20 minutes

Ingredients

- 2 Tbsp canola oil
- 4 small boneless, skinless chicken breasts
- 1 small white onion
- 4 small peaches
- 15 oz. can diced tomatoes
- 1/4 cup balsamic vinegar
- 3 Tbsp honey or compliant sweetener
- Side: veggies
- Side: spinach salad
- 1 gallon-size freezer baggie

Cooking Directions

1. Slice the onion.
2. Seed and slice the peaches.
3. In a large skillet, heat the canola oil, and brown both sides of the chicken breasts. Once browned, add the sliced onion, sliced peaches, diced tomatoes, balsamic vinegar and honey or compliant sweetener. Gently stir to combine.
4. Bring to bubbling and let cook over medium low heat for 10 to 12 minutes, or until chicken is cooked through. Flip the chicken pieces at least twice, while simmering.
5. Prepare veggies.
6. Prepare the salad.
7. Serve Peach & Balsamic Chicken Skillet with veggies and spinach salad.

Prepare to Freeze Directions

- Slice 1 onion.
- Seed and slice 4 peaches.
- To gallon-size plastic freezer baggie, add the following ingredients:
  - 4 small boneless, skinless chicken breasts
  - Salt and pepper
  - Sliced onions
  - Sliced peaches
  - 15 oz. can diced tomatoes
  - 1/4 cup balsamic vinegar
  - 3 Tbsp honey or compliant sweetener
- Remove as much air as possible and seal. Add label to baggie and freeze.

Freeze & Thaw Directions

Put baggie in the freezer and freeze up to 6 months in fridge freezer or 12 months in a deep freezer. Thaw in the fridge overnight, or a warm bowl of water for about 20 minutes, before transferring to the skillet for cooking as directed.

Shrimp Mango Curry

Yield: 4 servings
Prep Time: 10 minutes
Cook Time: 20 minutes

Ingredients

- 2 lbs. peeled deveined shrimp
- 1 Tbsp olive oil
- 4 green onions
- 1 tsp minced garlic
- 15 oz. can light coconut milk
- 2 Tbsp curry powder
- 1 tsp ground ginger
- 1 mango
- Salt and pepper
- Garnish: chopped cilantro
- Side: cauliflower rice
- Gallon-size freezer baggie

Cooking Directions

1. Cook the cauliflower rice, as directed.
2. Slice the green onions. Dice the mango.
3. In a large Dutch oven, heat the olive oil and saute the green onions and garlic for 30 seconds to 1 minute. Stir in the coconut milk, curry powder and ginger and bring to bubbling.
4. Add the shrimp and diced mango into the sauce. Let cook for 3 to 5 minutes, or until shrimp have turned pink (if they were raw). Reduce heat to low and cook for 10 minutes, allowing flavors to mingle. (If you don't plan to serve it right away, remove it from the heat and reheat, so the mangoes don't overcook.)
5. Serve Shrimp Mango Curry with cilantro garnish, over rice.

Prepare to Freeze Directions

- Slice the green onions. Dice 1 mango.
- To gallon-size plastic freezer baggie, add the following ingredients:
  - 2 lbs. peeled deveined shrimp
  - Sliced green onions
  - 1 tsp minced garlic
  - 2 Tbsp curry powder
  - 1 tsp ground ginger
  - Diced mango
  - Do NOT add canned coconut milk to the freezer baggie.
- Remove as much air as possible and seal. Add label to baggie and freeze.

Freeze & Thaw Directions

Put baggie in the freezer and freeze up to 6 months in fridge freezer or 12 months in a deep freezer. Thaw completely in the fridge overnight, or a warm bowl of water for about 20 minutes, before heating the olive oil to a Dutch oven and adding the shrimp, mango, canned coconut milk, and curry sauce to the Dutch oven or saucepan. Bring to bubbling and then simmer for 10 minutes.

Paleo Chicken Taco Salad

Yield: 4 servings
Prep Time: 15 minutes
Cook Time: 20 minutes

Ingredients

- 1 green bell pepper
- 1 orange bell pepper
- 1 small white onion
- 2 large boneless, skinless chicken breasts
- 1/4 cup lime juice
- 3 Tbsp homemade taco seasoning
- 2 Tbsp olive oil
- Salt and pepper
- 1/2 cup compliant vinaigrette salad dressing
- Garnish: guacamole
- Side: veggies
- 1 gallon-size freezer baggie
- About 1/2 cup compliant vinaigretee
- 4 cups Romaine lettuce leaves

Cooking Directions

1. Seed and slice the green and red bell peppers. Slice the onion.
2. Thinly slice the chicken breasts.
3. In a large bowl, toss together the bell pepper and onion slices, chicken slices, lime juice and taco seasoning.
4. Add the meat and veggies to large skillet with olive oil and saute for 8 to 10 minutes, or until chicken is cooked through and veggies have softened.
5. Prepare veggies.
6. Add Romaine leaves to serving plates, then top with cooked chicken and veggies and sprinkle vinaigrette salad dressing. Garnish with dollop of guacamole.
7. Serve Paleo Chicken Taco Salad with veggies.

Prepare to Freeze Directions

- Thinly slice 2 chicken breasts.
- Seed and slice 1 green bell pepper and 1 orange bell pepper. Slice 1 small white onion.
- To gallon-size plastic freezer baggie, add the following ingredients:
  - Sliced chicken breasts
  - Sliced green bell peppers
  - Sliced red bell peppers
  - Ssliced onion
  - 1/4 cup lime juice
  - 3 Tbsp homemade taco seasoning
- Remove as much air as you can and seal. Freeze up to 6 months in your fridge freezer or 12 months in a deep freezer.

Freeze & Thaw Directions

Put baggie in the freezer and freeze up to 6 months in fridge freezer or 12 months in a deep freezer. Thaw in the fridge overnight, or a warm bowl of water for about 20 minutes, before transferring to skillet and sauteing the chicken and veggies until cooked through. Prepare salad as directed.

Special Note: *Homemade taco seasoning mix recipe is here - www.5dollardinners.com/ homemade-taco-seasoning*

Flank Steak with Chimichurri

Yield: 4 servings
Prep Time: 15 minutes
Cook Time: 10 minutes

Ingredients

- 1 1/2 lb. flank steak
- 2 Tbsp coconut oil
- 1 tsp garlic powder
- 1 tsp ground cumin
- 1 tsp dried oregano
- Salt and pepper
- 2 Tbsp fresh parsley
- 2 Tbsp cilantro
- 1 tsp minced garlic
- 1 tsp minced onion
- 2 Tbsp olive oil
- 2 Tbsp vinegar
- Garnish: chimichurri sauce
- Side: cauliflower rice
- Side: veggies
- 1 gallon-size freezer baggie

Cooking Directions

1. In a small mixing bowl, whisk together the coconut oil, garlic powder, ground cumin and dried oregano and a few pinches of salt and pepper. *You might need to heat the coconut oil to get the rub to hold together.
2. Place the flank steak in baking dish and score with knife in criss-cross pattern. Pour or spread the oil-spice mixture over the top. Cover with plastic wrap and marinate in the fridge for at least 2 hours or overnight, ideally.
3. Cook the cauliflower rice, as directed.
4. Heat a large skillet or grill pan on the stovetop, then sear both sides of the flank steak for 30 seconds each side. Sear-saute for 1 to 2 more minutes per side, until cooked to your liking.

5. While the steak is cooking, make the chimichurri sauce. Add the following ingredients to small food processor and puree: parsley, fresh cilantro, minced garlic, minced onion, olive oil and vinegar.
6. Let rest for a few minutes, then slice against the grain and garnish with the homemade chimichurri.
7. Prepare the veggies.
8. Serve Flank Steak with Chimichurri and cauliflower rice and veggies.

Prepare to Freeze Directions

- In a small mixing bowl, whisk together 2 Tbsp coconut oil, 1 tsp garlic powder, 1 tsp ground cumin, 1 tsp dried oregano and a few pinches of salt and pepper. *You might need to heat the coconut oil to get the rub to hold together.
- To gallon-size plastic freezer baggie, add the following ingredients:
  - 1 1/2 lb. flank steak
  - Prepared steak marinade
  - Do NOT freeze the homemade chimichurri sauce ingredients.
- Remove as much air as posstovetsible and seal. Add label to baggie and freeze.

Freeze & Thaw Directions

Put baggie in the freezer and freeze up to 6 months in fridge freezer or 12 months in a deep freezer. Thaw completely in the fridge overnight, or a warm bowl of water for about 20 minutes, before transferring to the skillet or grill pan and searing as directed.

Freezer Meal Plan #1 - Recipes, Shopping Lists & Instructions

Cuban Chili

Greek Chicken Bake

Skillet Pork Chops with Mushrooms and Pearled Onions

Slow Cooker Beef Roast and Brussels Sprouts

Slow Cooker Chicken No-Tortilla Soup

Note: The following meal plans are written with 5 recipes that double to make a total of 10 meals. The shopping lists and instructions are written to make 2 meals worth of each recipe.

1. Cuban Chili

Yield: *4 servings*
Active Time: 15 minutes. Cook Time: 30 minutes

Recipe is written to make a single meal. Assembly Prep Directions & Shopping Lists will both contain directions and ingredients to make 2 meals, based on the number of servings you selected.

** This ingredient is used on the day you cook this meal. It is not added at the time you assemble and prepare your meals for the freezer.

Ingredients for Single Meal

- 1 - lb(s) ground beef
- 1 - Tbsp minced onion
- 1 - tsp garlic powder
- 1 - green bell pepper(s)
- 1 - 15 oz. can(s) diced tomatoes
- 1 - Tbsp chili powder
- 1 - tsp ground cumin
- 1 - tsp dried oregano
- 1/2 - tsp cinnamon
- 2 - cup(s) beef broth
- 1 - cup(s) raisins
- - Salt and pepper
- Side: - salad**
- 1 - gallon-size freezer baggie(s)

Cooking Directions for Single Meal

1. Open and drain the can of diced tomatoes.
2. Seed and chop the green bell pepper.
3. In a large saucepan, brown the ground beef with the minced onion and garlic powder. Drain and return to saucepan. Stir in the chopped bell pepper, diced tomatoes, chili powder, ground cumin, dried oregano, and cinnamon and saute for 5 minutes.
4. Stir in the beef broth and raisins and let simmer for 10 minutes to allow the flavors to mingle. Season with salt and pepper to taste.
5. Prepare the salad.
6. Serve Cuban Chili with salad.

Assembly Prep Directions for 2 Meals

- Brown 2 lbs. ground beef with 2 Tbsp minced onion and 2 tsp garlic powder. Let cool.
- Seed and chop 2 green bell peppers.
- Open and drain 2 cans of diced tomatoes.
- To each gallon-size plastic freezer baggie, add the following ingredients:
  - Half of the browned ground beef
  - Half of the diced tomatoes
  - Half of the chopped bell peppers
  - 1 Tbsp chili powder
  - 1 tsp ground cumin
  - 1 tsp dried oregano
  - 1/2 tsp cinnamon
  - 2 cups beef broth
  - 1 cup raisins
  - Salt and pepper
- Remove as much air as possible and seal. Add label to baggie and freeze.

Freeze & Thaw Instructions: *Put baggie in the freezer and freeze up to 6 months in fridge freezer or 12 months in a deep freezer. Thaw in the fridge overnight, or a warm bowl of water for about 20 minutes, before transferring all of the contents of the baggie into large saucepan or Dutch oven. Bring to bubbling and cook for 20 minutes.*

Special Notes: *Use unsweetened raisins for Paleo meal.*

Dairy-Free Modifications: *Recipe is dairy-free when served with dairy-free sides.*

Gluten-Free Modifications: *Recipe is gluten-free when served with gluten-free sides.*

2. Greek Chicken Bake

Yield: 4 servings
Active Time: 10 minutes. Cook Time: 45 minutes

Recipe is written to make a single meal. Assembly Prep Directions & Shopping Lists will both contain directions and ingredients to make 2 meals, based on the number of servings you selected.

** This ingredient is used on the day you cook this meal. It is not added at the time you assemble and prepare your meals for the freezer.

Ingredients for Single Meal

- 4 - small boneless chicken breasts
- - Salt and pepper
- 2 - cup(s) cherry tomatoes
- 1 - cup(s) can(s) artichoke hearts
- 1 - cup(s) green olives
- 2 - Tbsp olive oil
- 2 - Tbsp lemon juice
- 2 - tsp minced garlic
- 2 - tsp dried oregano
- Garnish: - feta cheese crumbles**
- Side: - salad**
- 1 - 9x13 disposable foil tray(s)

Cooking Directions for Single Meal

1. Preheat the oven to 400 F.
2. Drain the artichoke hearts, pat dry, and then quarter them.
3. In a small mixing bowl, whisk together the olive oil, lemon juice, minced garlic and oregano.
4. Place the chicken breasts into a 9x13-inch baking dish and sprinkle with a little salt and pepper. Add the cherry tomatoes, quartered artichoke hearts and olives around the chicken pieces. Pour the lemon juice marinade over the top.
5. Bake in the preheated oven for 45 minutes, or until chicken is cooked through. Sprinkle Feta cheese crumbles onto warm chicken bake, so they soften up. Omit garnish if Whole30/Paleo.
6. Prepare the salad.
7. Serve Greek Chicken Bake with salad.

Assembly Prep Directions for 2 Meals

- In a small mixing bowl, whisk together the 4 Tbsp olive oil, 4 Tbsp lemon juice, 4 tsp minced garlic and 4 tsp oregano.
- Drain 2 cups artichoke hearts, pat dry and then quarter them.
- To each disposable foil tray, add the following ingredients:
  - 4 small boneless chicken breasts
  - Salt and pepper
  - Half of the cherry tomatoes
  - Half of the quartered artichoke hearts
  - Half of the green olives
  - Half of the prepared Greek lemon marinade
- Cover tightly with foil or lid, add label to tray and freeze.

Freeze & Thaw Instructions: *Put tray in the freezer and freeze up to 6 months in fridge freezer or 12 months in a deep freezer. Thaw in the fridge overnight, or a warm shallow dish of water for about 20 minutes, before transferring to the oven and baking as directed.*

Dairy-Free Modifications: *Omit the Feta cheese crumbles for dairy-free & Paleo meal.*

Gluten-Free Modifications: *Recipe is gluten-free when served with gluten-free sides.*

3. Skillet Pork Chops with Mushrooms and Pearled Onions

Yield: 4 servings
Active Time: 10 minutes. Cook Time: 25 minutes

Recipe is written to make a single meal. Assembly Prep Directions & Shopping Lists will both contain directions and ingredients to make 2 meals, based on the number of servings you selected.

** This ingredient is used on the day you cook this meal. It is not added at the time you assemble and prepare your meals for the freezer.

Ingredients for Single Meal

- 4 - boneless pork chops
- - Salt and pepper
- 2 - Tbsp olive oil
- 8 - oz. baby bella mushrooms
- 10 - oz. bag(s) frozen pearled onions
- 1 - tsp dried thyme
- 1 - tsp dried basil
- Side: - salad**
- Side: - mashed cauliflower**
- 1 - gallon-size freezer baggie(s)

Cooking Directions for Single Meal

1. Heat the olive oil in skillet and saute the baby bella mushrooms and frozen pearled onions for 4 to 5 minutes. Pour them out into a bowl and set aside.
2. In the same skillet, brown the pork chops for 2 minutes on each side. Add the sauteed mushrooms and pearled onions back into the skillet and add the dried thyme and basil. Stir to combine, reduce heat and simmer for 5 to 8 minutes, or until pork chops are cooked through.
3. Prepare the salad.
4. Prepare the mashed cauliflower.
5. Serve Skillet Pork Chops with Mushrooms and Pearled Onions with salad and dinner rolls.

Assembly Prep Directions for 2 Meals

- To each gallon-size plastic freezer baggie, add the following ingredients:
  - 4 boneless pork chops
  - Salt and pepper
  - 2 Tbsp olive oil
  - 8 oz. baby bella sliced mushrooms
  - 1 - 10 oz. bag frozen pearled onions
  - 1 tsp dried thyme
  - 1 tsp dried basil
- Remove as much air as possible and seal. Add label to baggie and freeze.

Freeze & Thaw Instructions: *Put baggie in the freezer and freeze up to 6 months in fridge freezer or 12 months in a deep freezer. Thaw in the fridge overnight, or a warm bowl of water for about 20 minutes, before transferring the veggies to a skillet and sauteeing. Remove veggies from pan. Then brown the pork chops on both sides, add the veggies back into the pan, and saute until the pork chops are cooked through.*

Dairy-Free Modifications: *Recipe is dairy-free when served with dairy-free sides.*

Gluten-Free Modifications: *Recipe is gluten-free when served with gluten-free sides.*

4. Slow Cooker Beef Roast and Brussels Sprouts

Yield: 4 servings

Active Time: 10 minutes. Cook Time: 8 hours in slow cooker

Recipe is written to make a single meal. Assembly Prep Directions & Shopping Lists will both contain directions and ingredients to make 2 meals, based on the number of servings you selected.

** This ingredient is used on the day you cook this meal. It is not added at the time you assemble and prepare your meals for the freezer.

Ingredients for Single Meal

- 2 - lb(s) beef chuck roast
- - Salt and pepper
- 4 - whole carrots
- 1 - small yellow onion(s)
- 20 - Brussels sprouts
- 1 - tsp minced garlic
- 1 - cup(s) beef broth
- Side: - salad**
- 1 - gallon-size freezer baggie(s)

Cooking Directions for Single Meal

1. Peel and cut the whole carrots into 1-inch pieces. Dice the yellow onion into 1/2-inch pieces.
2. Place the beef roast into the base of the slow cooker and season with salt and pepper. Sprinkle the carrot pieces, onion pieces, Brussels sprouts, minced garlic and beef broth over the roast.
3. Set the slow cooker on low and cook for 8 hours. Once finished cooking, slice the beef or shred the beef with 2 forks and mix into the sauce. Spoon out the vegetables onto serving plates. If desired, make gravy with flour or coconut flour (keto).
4. Prepare salad.
5. Serve Slow Cooker Beef Roast and Brussels Sprouts with side salad.

Assembly Prep Directions for 2 Meals

- Peel and cut 8 whole carrots into 1-inch pieces. Dice 2 small yellow onions into 1/2-inch pieces
- To each gallon-size plastic freezer baggie, add the following ingredients:
  - 2 lb. beef chuck roast
  - Salt and pepper
  - Half of the carrot pieces
  - Half of the diced onion
  - 20 Brussels Sprouts
  - 1 tsp minced garlic
  - 1 cup beef broth
- Remove as much air as possible and seal. Add label to baggie and freeze.

Freeze & Thaw Instructions: *Put baggie in the freezer and freeze up to 6 months in fridge freezer or 12 months in a deep freezer. Thaw in the fridge overnight, or a warm bowl of water for about 20 minutes, before transferring to the slow cooker and cooking on low for 8 hours.*

Dairy-Free Modifications: *Recipe is dairy-free when served with dairy-free sides.*

Gluten-Free Modifications: *Recipe is gluten-free when served with gluten-free sides.*

5. Slow Cooker Chicken No-Tortilla Soup

Yield: 4 servings
Active Time: 10 minutes. Cook Time: 8 hour in slow cooker

Recipe is written to make a single meal. Assembly Prep Directions & Shopping Lists will both contain directions and ingredients to make 2 meals, based on the number of servings you selected.

** This ingredient is used on the day you cook this meal. It is not added at the time you assemble and prepare your meals for the freezer.

Ingredients for Single Meal

- 4 - large boneless chicken breasts
- 1 - red bell pepper(s)
- 1 - 15 oz. can(s) tomato sauce
- 1 - 15 oz can(s) petite diced tom
- 1 - Tbsp chili powder
- 1 - tsp ground cumin
- 1 - tsp garlic powder
- 1 - tsp onion powder
- 2 - cup(s) chicken or vegetable stock
- - Salt and pepper
- Garnish: - avocado slices**
- Side: - salad or veggies**
- 1 - gallon-size freezer baggie(s)

Cooking Directions for Single Meal

1. Seed and dice the red bell pepper.
2. To the slow cooker, add the chicken, tomato sauce, diced tomatoes, chili powder, cumin, garlic powder, onion powder, red bell pepper, and chicken or vegetable stock. Set slow cooker on low and cook for 8 hours.
3. Before serving, use 2 forks to pull the chicken apart in the soup. Then ladle soup into bowls and add the avocado slices into each bowl.
4. Serve Slow Cooker Chicken No-Tortilla Soup with avocado slices.

Assembly Prep Directions for 2 Meals

- Seed and dice 2 red bell peppers.
- Open 2 cans of tomato sauce.
- Open 2 cans of diced tomatoes.
- To each gallon-size plastic freezer baggie, add the following ingredients:
  - 4 boneless, skinless chicken breasts
  - Half of the diced red bell pepper
  - Half of the diced tomatoes
  - Half of the tomato sauce
  - 1 Tbsp chili powder
  - 2 cups chicken or vegetable stock
  - 1 tsp ground cumin
  - 1 tsp garlic powder
  - 1 tsp onion powder
- Remove as much air as possible and seal. Add label to baggie and freeze.

Freeze & Thaw Instructions: *Put baggie in the freezer and freeze up to 6 months in fridge freezer or 12 months in a deep freezer. Thaw in the fridge overnight, or a warm bowl of water for about 20 minutes, before transferring to the slow cooker and cooking on low for 8 hours. Once cooked, shred the chicken into the soup, ladle into bowls and garnish.*

Dairy-Free Modifications: *Recipe is dairy-free when served with dairy-free sides.*

Gluten-Free Modifications: *Recipe is gluten-free when served with gluten-free sides.*

Complete Shopping List by Recipe

1. Cuban Chili

- ☐ 2 lb(s) ground beef
- ☐ 2 Tbsp minced onion
- ☐ 2 tsp garlic powder
- ☐ 2 green bell pepper(s)
- ☐ 2 - 15 oz. can(s) diced tomatoes
- ☐ 2 Tbsp chili powder
- ☐ 2 tsp ground cumin
- ☐ 2 tsp dried oregano
- ☐ 1 tsp cinnamon
- ☐ 4 cup(s) beef broth
- ☐ 2 cup(s) unsweetened raisins
- ☐ Salt and pepper
- ☐ **Side:** salad
- ☐ 2 gallon-size freezer baggie(s)

2. Greek Chicken Bake

- ☐ 8 small boneless chicken breasts
- ☐ Salt and pepper
- ☐ 4 cup(s) cherry tomatoes
- ☐ 2 cup(s) can(s) artichoke hearts
- ☐ 2 cup(s) green olives
- ☐ 4 Tbsp olive oil
- ☐ 4 Tbsp lemon juice
- ☐ 4 tsp minced garlic
- ☐ 4 tsp dried oregano
- ☐ **Garnish:** feta cheese crumbles
- ☐ **Side:** salad
- ☐ 2 - 9x13 disposable foil tray(s)

3. Skillet Pork Chops with Mushrooms and Pearled Onions

- ☐ 8 boneless pork chops
- ☐ Salt and pepper
- ☐ 4 Tbsp olive oil
- ☐ 2 - 8 oz. baby bella mushrooms
- ☐ 2 - 10 oz. bag(s) frozen pearled onions
- ☐ 2 tsp dried thyme
- ☐ 2 tsp dried basil
- ☐ **Side:** salad
- ☐ **Side:** mashed cauliflower
- ☐ 2 gallon-size freezer baggie(s)

4. Slow Cooker Beef Roast and Brussels Sprouts

- ☐ 4 lb(s) beef chuck roast
- ☐ Salt and pepper
- ☐ 8 whole carrots
- ☐ 2 small yellow onion(s)
- ☐ 40 Brussels sprouts
- ☐ 2 tsp minced garlic
- ☐ 2 cup(s) beef broth
- ☐ **Side:** salad
- ☐ 2 gallon-size freezer baggie(s)

5. Slow Cooker Chicken No-Tortilla Soup

- ☐ 8 large boneless chicken breasts
- ☐ 2 red bell pepper(s)
- ☐ 2 - 15 oz. can(s) tomato sauce
- ☐ 2 - 15 oz can(s) petite diced tom
- ☐ 2 Tbsp chili powder
- ☐ 2 tsp ground cumin
- ☐ 2 tsp garlic powder
- ☐ 2 tsp onion powder
- ☐ 4 cup(s) chicken or vegetable stock
- ☐ Salt and pepper
- ☐ **Garnish:** avocado slices
- ☐ **Side:** salad or veggies
- ☐ 2 gallon-size freezer baggie(s)

Complete Shopping List by Store Section/Category

Meat

- ☐ 2 lb(s) ground beef
- ☐ 8 small boneless chicken breasts
- ☐ 8 boneless pork chops
- ☐ 4 lb(s) beef chuck roast
- ☐ 8 large boneless chicken breasts

Produce

- ☐ 2 green bell pepper(s)
- ☐ **Side:** salad
- ☐ 4 cup(s) cherry tomatoes
- ☐ 4 Tbsp lemon juice
- ☐ 2 - 8 oz. baby bella mushrooms
- ☐ **Side:** mashed cauliflower
- ☐ 8 whole carrots
- ☐ 2 small yellow onion(s)
- ☐ 40 Brussels sprouts
- ☐ 2 red bell pepper(s)
- ☐ avocado slices
- ☐ **Side:** salad or veggies

Pantry Staples - Canned, Boxed

- ☐ 2 - 15 oz. can(s) diced tomatoes
- ☐ 6 cup(s) beef broth
- ☐ 2 cup(s) unsweentened raisins
- ☐ 2 cup(s) can(s) artichoke hearts
- ☐ 2 cup(s) green olives
- ☐ 2 - 15 oz. can(s) tomato sauce
- ☐ 2 - 15 oz can(s) petite diced tom
- ☐ 4 cup(s) chicken or vegetable stock

Sauces/Condiments

- ☐ 8 Tbsp olive oil

Spices

- ☐ 2 Tbsp minced onion
- ☐ 4 tsp garlic powder
- ☐ 4 Tbsp chili powder
- ☐ 4 tsp ground cumin
- ☐ 6 tsp dried oregano
- ☐ 1 tsp cinnamon
- ☐ Salt and pepper
- ☐ 6 tsp minced garlic
- ☐ 2 tsp dried thyme
- ☐ 2 tsp dried basil
- ☐ 2 tsp onion powder

Dairy/Frozen

- ☐ **Garnish:** feta cheese crumbles
- ☐ 2 - 10 oz. bag(s) frozen pearled onions

Supplies

- ☐ **Side:** 8 gallon-size freezer baggie(s)
- ☐ **Side:** 2 - 9x13 disposable foil tray(s)

Freezer Meal Prep Day Shopping List by Recipe

Note: This shopping list doesn't include any side dish items like rice, dinner rolls, veggies or salad.

**In addition to a shopping list for prep day, this list could be used to help you organize ingredients on your counter before you begin preparing the meals for the freezer.

1. Cuban Chili

- ☐ 2 lb(s) ground beef
- ☐ 2 Tbsp minced onion
- ☐ 2 tsp garlic powder
- ☐ 2 green bell pepper(s)
- ☐ 2 - 15 oz. can(s) diced tomatoes
- ☐ 2 Tbsp chili powder
- ☐ 2 tsp ground cumin
- ☐ 2 tsp dried oregano
- ☐ 1 tsp cinnamon
- ☐ 4 cup(s) beef broth
- ☐ 2 cup(s) unsweetened raisins
- ☐ Salt and pepper
- ☐ 2 gallon-size freezer baggie(s)

2. Greek Chicken Bake

- ☐ 8 small boneless chicken breasts
- ☐ Salt and pepper
- ☐ 4 cup(s) cherry tomatoes
- ☐ 2 cup(s) can(s) artichoke hearts
- ☐ 2 cup(s) green olives
- ☐ 4 Tbsp olive oil
- ☐ 4 Tbsp lemon juice
- ☐ 4 tsp minced garlic
- ☐ 4 tsp dried oregano
- ☐ 2 - 9x13 disposable foil tray(s)

3. Skillet Pork Chops with Mushrooms and Pearled Onions

- ☐ 8 boneless pork chops
- ☐ Salt and pepper
- ☐ 4 Tbsp olive oil
- ☐ 2 - 8 oz. baby bella mushrooms
- ☐ 2 - 10 oz. bag(s) frozen pearled onions

- ☐ 2 tsp dried thyme
- ☐ 2 tsp dried basil
- ☐ 2 gallon-size freezer baggie(s)

4. Slow Cooker Beef Roast and Brussels Sprouts

- ☐ 4 lb(s) beef chuck roast
- ☐ Salt and pepper
- ☐ 8 whole carrots
- ☐ 2 small yellow onion(s)
- ☐ 40 Brussels sprouts
- ☐ 2 tsp minced garlic
- ☐ 2 cup(s) beef broth
- ☐ 2 gallon-size freezer baggie(s)

5. Slow Cooker Chicken No-Tortilla Soup

- ☐ 8 large boneless chicken breasts
- ☐ 2 red bell pepper(s)
- ☐ 2 - 15 oz. can(s) tomato sauce
- ☐ 2 - 15 oz can(s) petite diced tom
- ☐ 2 Tbsp chili powder
- ☐ 2 tsp ground cumin
- ☐ 2 tsp garlic powder
- ☐ 2 tsp onion powder
- ☐ 4 cup(s) chicken or vegetable stock
- ☐ Salt and pepper
- ☐ 2 gallon-size freezer baggie(s)

Freezer Meal Prep Day Shopping List by Store Section/Category

Note: This shopping list doesn't include any side dish items like fruit, dinner rolls, veggies or salad.

Meat

- ☐ 2 lb(s) ground beef
- ☐ 8 small boneless chicken breasts
- ☐ 8 boneless pork chops
- ☐ 4 lb(s) beef chuck roast
- ☐ 8 large boneless chicken breasts

Produce

- ☐ 2 green bell pepper(s)
- ☐ 4 cup(s) cherry tomatoes
- ☐ 4 Tbsp lemon juice
- ☐ 2 - 8 oz. baby bella mushrooms
- ☐ 8 whole carrots
- ☐ 2 small yellow onion(s)
- ☐ 40 Brussels sprouts
- ☐ 2 red bell pepper(s)

Pantry Staples - Canned, Boxed

- ☐ 2 - 15 oz. can(s) diced tomatoes
- ☐ 6 cup(s) beef broth
- ☐ 2 cup(s) raisins
- ☐ 2 cup(s) can(s) artichoke hearts
- ☐ 2 cup(s) green olives
- ☐ 2 - 15 oz. can(s) tomato sauce
- ☐ 2 - 15 oz can(s) petite diced tom
- ☐ 4 cup(s) chicken or vegetable stock

Sauces/Condiments

- ☐ 8 Tbsp olive oil

Spices

- ☐ 2 Tbsp minced onion
- ☐ 4 tsp garlic powder
- ☐ 4 Tbsp chili powder
- ☐ 4 tsp ground cumin
- ☐ 6 tsp dried oregano
- ☐ 1 tsp cinnamon
- ☐ Salt and pepper
- ☐ 6 tsp minced garlic
- ☐ 2 tsp dried thyme
- ☐ 2 tsp dried basil
- ☐ 2 tsp onion powder

Dairy/Frozen

- ☐ 2 - 10 oz. bag(s) frozen pearled onions

Supplies

- ☐ 8x gallon-size freezer baggie(s)
- ☐ 2 - 9x13 disposable foil tray(s)

Meal Assembly Instructions

☐ Label your bags/foil with printable labels or sharpie.
☐ Pull out all the ingredients into a central location or into stations.

Pre-Cook & Chop Instructions

☐ Brown 2 lbs. ground beef with 2 Tbsp minced onion and 2 tsp garlic powder. Let cool.
☐ Seed and chop 2 green bell peppers.
☐ Seed and dice 2 red bell peppers.
☐ Peel and cut 8 whole carrots into 1-inch pieces. Dice 2 small yellow onions into 1/2-inch pieces.
☐ In a small mixing bowl, whisk together the 4 Tbsp olive oil, 4 Tbsp lemon juice, 4 tsp minced garlic and 4 tsp oregano.
☐ Open and drain 2 cans of diced tomatoes.
☐ Open 2 cans of tomato sauce.
☐ Open 2 cans of diced tomatoes.
☐ Drain 2 cups artichoke hearts, pat dry and then quarter them.

The Assembly Prep should take between 30 to 35 minutes.

Assembly by Recipe (Set Out on the Counter)

If you prefer to load your freezer baggies and trays one recipe at a time, you can follow the below instructions.

Cuban Chili

To each gallon-size plastic freezer baggie, add the following ingredients:

- Half of the browned ground beef
- Half of the diced tomatoes
- Half of the chopped bell peppers
- 1 Tbsp chili powder
- 1 tsp ground cumin
- 1 tsp dried oregano
- 1/2 tsp cinnamon
- 2 cups beef broth
- 1 cup raisins
- Salt and pepper

Remove as much air as possible and seal. Add label to baggie and freeze.

Greek Chicken Bake

To each disposable foil tray, add the following ingredients:

- 4 small boneless chicken breasts
- Salt and pepper
- Half of the cherry tomatoes
- Half of the quartered artichoke hearts
- Half of the green olives
- Half of the prepared Greek lemon marinade

Cover tightly with foil or lid, add label to tray and freeze.

Skillet Pork Chops with Mushrooms and Pearled Onions

To each gallon-size plastic freezer baggie, add the following ingredients:

- 4 boneless pork chops
- Salt and pepper
- 2 Tbsp olive oil
- 8 oz. baby bella sliced mushrooms
- 1 - 10 oz. bag frozen pearled onions
- 1 tsp dried thyme
- 1 tsp dried basil

Remove as much air as possible and seal. Add label to baggie and freeze.

Slow Cooker Beef Roast and Brussels Sprouts

To each gallon-size plastic freezer baggie, add the following ingredients:

- 2 lb. beef chuck roast
- Salt and pepper
- Half of the carrot pieces
- Half of the diced onion
- 20 Brussels Sprouts
- 1 tsp minced garlic
- 1 cup beef broth

Remove as much air as possible and seal. Add label to baggie and freeze.

Slow Cooker Chicken No-Tortilla Soup

To each gallon-size plastic freezer baggie, add the following ingredients:

- 4 boneless, skinless chicken breasts
- Half of the diced red bell pepper
- Half of the diced tomatoes
- Half of the tomato sauce
- 1 Tbsp chili powder
- 2 cups chicken or vegetable stock
- 1 tsp ground cumin
- 1 tsp garlic powder
- 1 tsp onion powder

Remove as much air as possible and seal. Add label to baggie and freeze.

Freezer Meal Plan #2 - Recipes, Shopping Lists & Instructions

New Mexican Chicken Lettuce Wraps

Paleo Chicken Taco Salad

Paleo Minestrone Soup

Slow Cooker Lemon & Dill Salmon

Slow Cooker Salsa Verde Shredded Pork

Note: The following meal plans are written with 5 recipes that double to make a total of 10 meals. The shopping lists and instructions are written to make 2 meals worth of each recipe.

1. New Mexican Chicken Lettuce Wraps

Yield: 4 servings
Active Time: 10 minutes. Cook Time: 8 hours in slow cooker

Recipe is written to make a single meal. Assembly Prep Directions & Shopping Lists will both contain directions and ingredients to make 2 meals, based on the number of servings you selected.

** This ingredient is used on the day you cook this meal. It is not added at the time you assemble and prepare your meals for the freezer.

Ingredients for Single Meal

- 3 - large boneless chicken breasts
- 1 - cup(s) red salsa
- 1 - 4 oz. can(s) green chiles
- 1 - Tbsp minced onion
- 1 - Tbsp ground cumin
- 1 - tsp garlic powder
- - Salt and pepper
- Garnish: - chopped cilantro**
- Side: - lettuce leaves**
- Side: - veggies**
- 1 - gallon-size freezer baggie(s)

Cooking Directions for Single Meal

1. Place the chicken breasts into the base of the slow cooker and add the red salsa, green chiles, minced onion, ground cumin, garlic powder and salt and pepper.
2. Set the slow cooker on low and cook for 8 hours. Once finished cooking, shred the chicken with 2 forks and mix into the sauce.
3. Spoon the shredded chicken into lettuce leaves and make lettuce wraps.
4. Prepare veggies.
5. Serve New Mexican Chicken Lettuce Wraps with veggies.

Assembly Prep Directions for 2 Meals

- To each gallon-size plastic freezer baggie, add the following ingredients:
  - 3 large boneless chicken breasts
  - 1 cup red salsa
  - 1 - 4 oz. can green chiles
  - 1 Tbsp minced onion
  - 1 Tbsp ground cumin
  - 1 tsp garlic powder
  - Salt and pepper
- Remove as much air as possible and seal. Add label to baggie and freeze.

Freeze & Thaw Instructions: *Put baggie in the freezer and freeze up to 6 months in fridge freezer or 12 months in a deep freezer. Thaw in the fridge overnight, or a warm bowl of water for about 20 minutes, before transferring to a slow cooker and cooking as directed.*

Dairy-Free Modifications: *Recipe is dairy-free when served with dairy-free sides.*

Gluten-Free Modifications: *Recipe is gluten-free when served with gluten-free sides.*

2. Paleo Chicken Taco Salad

Yield: 4 servings
Active Time: 15 minutes. Cook Time: 20 minutes

Recipe is written to make a single meal. Assembly Prep Directions & Shopping Lists will both contain directions and ingredients to make 2 meals, based on the number of servings you selected.

** This ingredient is used on the day you cook this meal. It is not added at the time you assemble and prepare your meals for the freezer.

Ingredients for Single Meal

- 1 - green bell pepper(s)
- 1 - orange bell pepper(s)
- 1 - small white onion(s)
- 2 - large boneless chicken breasts
- 1/4 - cup(s) lime juice
- 1 - packet(s) taco seasoning
- 2 - Tbsp olive oil**
- - Salt and pepper**
- 1/2 - cup(s) Vinaigrette salad dressing**
- Garnish: - guacamole**
- Side: - veggies**
- 1 - gallon-size freezer baggie(s)

Cooking Directions for Single Meal

1. Seed and slice the green and red bell peppers. Slice the onion.
2. Thinly slice the chicken breasts.
3. In a large bowl, toss together the bell pepper and onion slices, chicken slices, lime juice and taco seasoning.
4. Add the meat and veggies to large skillet with olive oil and saute for 8 to 10 minutes, or until chicken is cooked through and veggies have softened.
5. Prepare veggies.
6. Add Romaine leaves to serving plates, then top with cooked chicken and veggies and sprinkle vinaigrette salad dressing. Garnish with dollop of guacamole.
7. Serve Paleo Chicken Taco Salad with veggies.

Assembly Prep Directions for 2 Meals

- Thinly slice 4 chicken breasts.
- Seed and slice 2 green bell peppers and 2 red bell peppers. Slice 2 small white onions.
- To each gallon-size plastic freezer baggie, add the following ingredients:
  - Half of the sliced chicken breasts
  - Half of the sliced green bell peppers
  - Half of the sliced red bell peppers
  - Half of the sliced onion
  - 1/4 cup lime juice
  - 1 packet taco seasoning
- Remove as much air as you can and seal. Freeze up to 6 months in your fridge freezer or 12 months in a deep freezer.

Freeze & Thaw Instructions: *Put baggie in the freezer and freeze up to 6 months in fridge freezer or 12 months in a deep freezer. Thaw in the fridge overnight, or a warm bowl of water for about 20 minutes, before transferring to skillet and sauteing the chicken and veggies until cooked through. Prepare salad as directed.*

Special Notes: *Be sure to use keto friendly guacamole, dressing and taco seasoning. Homemade taco seasoning mix on 5DollarDinners.com here: www.5dollardinners.com/homemade-taco-seasoning*

Dairy-Free Modifications: *Recipe is dairy-free when served with dairy-free sides.*

Gluten-Free Modifications: *Recipe is gluten-free when served with gluten-free sides.*

3. Paleo Minestrone Soup

Yield: 4 servings
Active Time: 20 minutes. Cook Time: 30 minutes

Recipe is written to make a single meal. Assembly Prep Directions & Shopping Lists will both contain directions and ingredients to make 2 meals, based on the number of servings you selected.

** This ingredient is used on the day you cook this meal. It is not added at the time you assemble and prepare your meals for the freezer.

Ingredients for Single Meal

- 2 - Tbsp olive oil
- 1 - small white onion(s)
- 2 - celery
- 2 - garlic cloves
- 4 - whole carrots
- 1/2 - lb(s) green beans
- 2 - medium zucchini
- 1 - 15 oz. can(s) tomato sauce
- 1 - Tbsp Italian seasoning
- 6 - cup(s) chicken or vegetable stock
- - Salt and pepper
- Side: - salad**
- 1 - gallon-size freezer baggie(s)

Cooking Directions for Single Meal

1. In a large saucepan, heat the olive oil and saute the onion, celery, garlic and carrots for 4 to 5 minutes. Stir in the green beans, zucchini, tomato sauce, Italian seasoning and chicken stock. Bring to bubbling.
2. Remove soup from the heat and prepare to spoon into serving bowls.
3. Serve Paleo Minestrone Soup with and side salad.

Assembly Prep Directions for 2 Meals

- Chop 2 white onions.
  Peel and chop 8 whole carrots.
  Slice 4 celery stalks.
  Trim 1 lb. green beans.
  Thinly slice 4 medium zucchini.
  Open 2 cans of tomato sauce.
- To each gallon-size plastic freezer baggie, add the following ingredients:
  ○ Half of the chopped onion
  ○ Half of the chopped celery
  ○ 2 garlic cloves, crushed
  ○ Half of the chopped carrots
  ○ Half of the trimmed green beans
  ○ Half of the sliced zucchini
  ○ 1 - 15 oz. can tomato sauce
  ○ 1 Tbsp Italian seasoning blend
  ○ 6 cups chicken or vegetable stock
- Remove as much air as possible and seal. Add label to baggie and freeze.

Freeze & Thaw Instructions: *Put baggie in the freezer and freeze up to 6 months in fridge freezer or 12 months in a deep freezer. Thaw in a warm bowl of water for about 20 minutes, before transferring all the ingredients to a large saucepan or stockpot. Reheat the soup and add pasta at end of cooking as directed.*

Dairy-Free Modifications: *Recipe is dairy-free when served with dairy-free sides.*

Gluten-Free Modifications: *Recipe is gluten-free when served with gluten-free sides.*

4. Slow Cooker Lemon & Dill Salmon

Yield: 4 servings
Active Time: 10 minutes. Cook Time: 1 hours on high

Recipe is written to make a single meal. Assembly Prep Directions & Shopping Lists will both contain directions and ingredients to make 2 meals, based on the number of servings you selected.

** This ingredient is used on the day you cook this meal. It is not added at the time you assemble and prepare your meals for the freezer.

Ingredients for Single Meal

- 1 - lb(s) salmon fillet
- - Salt and pepper
- 2 - tsp lemon juice
- 2 - tsp fresh dill
- Side: - veggies**
- Side: - cauliflower rice**
- 1 - gallon-size freezer baggie(s)

Cooking Directions for Single Meal

1. Place a large piece of parchment paper into the base of the slow cooker. The parchment paper is to make it easier to lift the salmon out of the slow cooker after it cooks.
2. Place the 4 salmon fillets flat on the parchment paper, skin side down. Sprinkle each with little salt and pepper over the top. Drizzle lemon juice over the salmon pieces. Place fresh chopped dill sprigs on salmon.
3. Set on high and cook for 1 hour.
4. Cook cauliflower rice as directed on package.
5. Prepare veggies, as needed.
6. Once salmon is cooked, carefully lift it out of the slow cooker onto a shallow serving dish. Remove skin and serve.
7. Serve Lemon & Dill Salmon with cauliflower rice and veggies.

Assembly Prep Directions for 2 Meals

- Cut 2 lbs. salmon into 8 - 1/4 lb. fillets.
- Halve 4 lemons.
- Finely chop 4 tsp fresh dill.
- To each gallon-size plastic freezer baggie, add the following ingredients:
  - Half of the salmon fillets
  - Salt and pepper
  - Juice from 2 lemons
  - Half of the chopped dill
- Remove as much air as possible and seal. Add label to baggie and freeze.

Freeze & Thaw Instructions: *Put baggie in the freezer and freeze up to 6 months in fridge freezer or 12 months in a deep freezer. Thaw in the fridge overnight, or a warm bowl of water for about 20 minutes, before transferring to the slow cooker lined with parchment paper, and cooking on high for 1 hour.*

Dairy-Free Modifications: *Recipe is dairy-free when served with dairy-free sides.*

Gluten-Free Modifications: *Recipe is gluten-free when served with gluten-free sides.*

5. Slow Cooker Salsa Verde Shredded Pork

Yield: 4 servings
Active Time: 10 minutes. Cook Time: 8 hours in slow cooker

Recipe is written to make a single meal. Assembly Prep Directions & Shopping Lists will both contain directions and ingredients to make 2 meals, based on the number of servings you selected.

** This ingredient is used on the day you cook this meal. It is not added at the time you assemble and prepare your meals for the freezer.

Ingredients for Single Meal

- 2 - lb(s) pork shoulder roast
- 1 - tsp garlic powder
- 1 - tsp ground cumin
- - Salt and pepper
- 1 1/2 - cup(s) salsa verde sauce
- 1 - large jalapeño(s)
- 3 - cup(s) cauliflower rice**
- 1 - cup(s) shredded Monterrey Jack cheese**
- Garnish: - sour cream**
- Topping: - cilantro or avocado chunks**
- Side: - veggies**
- 1 - gallon-size freezer baggie(s)

Cooking Directions for Single Meal

1. Seed and dice the jalapeno(s).
2. Place the pork roast into the base of the slow cooker and sprinkle the garlic powder, ground cumin, salt and pepper on top of the pork roast. Pour the salsa verde and add the diced jalapenos on top.
3. Set the slow cooker on low and cook for 8 hours.
4. Just before serving, prepare the cauliflower rice.
5. Once the cooking time is complete, shred the pork with 2 forks and remove from the slow cooker with slotted spoon when ready to serve. Spoon the shredded pork onto the cauliflower rice and add preferred toppings.
6. Prepare veggies.
7. Serve Slow Cooker Salsa Verde Shredded Pork with veggies and preferred toppings.

Assembly Prep Directions for 2 Meals

- Remove the seeds and dice 2 jalapenos.
- To each gallon-size plastic freezer baggie, add the following ingredients:
  - 2 lb. pork shoulder roast
  - 1 tsp garlic powder
  - 1 tsp ground cumin
  - Salt and pepper
  - 1 1/2 cups salsa verde sauce
  - Half of the diced jalapeno into each bag
- Remove as much air as possible and seal. Add label to baggie and freeze.

Freeze & Thaw Instructions: *Put baggie in the freezer and freeze up to 6 months in fridge freezer or 12 months in a deep freezer. Thaw in a warm bowl of water for about 20 minutes, before transferring to the slow cooker and cooking on low for 8 hours.*

Dairy-Free Modifications: *Omit cheese or sour cream garnish.*

Gluten-Free Modifications: *Recipe is gluten-free when served with gluten-free sides.*

Complete Shopping List by Recipe

1. New Mexican Chicken Lettuce Wraps

- ☐ 6 large boneless chicken breasts
- ☐ 2 cup(s) red salsa
- ☐ 2 - 4 oz. can(s) green chiles
- ☐ 2 Tbsp minced onion
- ☐ 2 Tbsp ground cumin
- ☐ 2 tsp garlic powder
- ☐ Salt and pepper
- ☐ **Garnish:** chopped cilantro
- ☐ **Side:** lettuce leaves
- ☐ **Side:** veggies
- ☐ 2 gallon-size freezer baggie(s)

2. Paleo Chicken Taco Salad

- ☐ 2 green bell pepper(s)
- ☐ 2 orange bell pepper(s)
- ☐ 2 small white onion(s)
- ☐ 4 large boneless chicken breasts
- ☐ 1/2 cup(s) lime juice
- ☐ 2 packet(s) taco seasoning
- ☐ 4 Tbsp olive oil
- ☐ Salt and pepper
- ☐ 1 cup(s) Vinaigrette salad dressing
- ☐ **Garnish:** guacamole
- ☐ **Side:** veggies
- ☐ 2 gallon-size freezer baggie(s)

3. Paleo Minestrone Soup

- ☐ 4 Tbsp olive oil
- ☐ 2 small white onion(s)
- ☐ 4 celery
- ☐ 4 garlic cloves
- ☐ 8 whole carrots
- ☐ 1 lb(s) green beans
- ☐ 4 medium zucchini
- ☐ 2 - 15 oz. can(s) tomato sauce
- ☐ 2 Tbsp Italian seasoning
- ☐ 12 cup(s) chicken or vegetable stock
- ☐ Salt and pepper
- ☐ **Side:** salad
- ☐ 2 gallon-size freezer baggie(s)

4. Slow Cooker Lemon & Dill Salmon

- ☐ 2 lb(s) salmon fillet
- ☐ Salt and pepper
- ☐ 4 tsp lemon juice
- ☐ 4 tsp fresh dill
- ☐ **Side:** veggies
- ☐ **Side:** cauliflower rice
- ☐ 2 gallon-size freezer baggie(s)

5. Slow Cooker Salsa Verde Shredded Pork

- ☐ 4 lb(s) pork shoulder roast
- ☐ 2 tsp garlic powder
- ☐ 2 tsp ground cumin
- ☐ Salt and pepper
- ☐ 3 cup(s) salsa verde sauce
- ☐ 2 large jalapeño(s)
- ☐ **Side:** 6 cup(s) cauliflower rice
- ☐ **Garnish:** 2 cup(s) shredded Monterrey Jack cheese
- ☐ **Garnish:** sour cream
- ☐ **Garnish:** cilantro or avocado chunks
- ☐ **Side:** veggies
- ☐ 2 gallon-size freezer baggie(s)

Complete Shopping List by Store Section/Category

Meat

- ☐ 10 large boneless chicken breasts
- ☐ 2 lb(s) salmon fillet
- ☐ 4 lb(s) pork shoulder roast

Produce

- ☐ **Garnish:** chopped cilantro
- ☐ **Side:** lettuce leaves
- ☐ **Side:** veggies
- ☐ 2 green bell pepper(s)
- ☐ 2 orange bell pepper(s)
- ☐ 4 small white onion(s)
- ☐ 1/2 cup(s) lime juice
- ☐ **Side:** guacamole
- ☐ 4 celery
- ☐ 8 whole carrots
- ☐ 1 lb(s) green beans
- ☐ 4 medium zucchini
- ☐ **Side:** salad
- ☐ 4 tsp lemon juice
- ☐ 4 tsp fresh dill
- ☐ 2 large jalapeño(s)
- ☐ **Side:** cilantro or avocado chunks

Pantry Staples - Canned, Boxed

- ☐ 2 cup(s) red salsa
- ☐ 2 - 4 oz. can(s) green chiles
- ☐ 1 cup(s) Vinaigrette salad dressing
- ☐ 2 - 15 oz. can(s) tomato sauce
- ☐ 12 cup(s) chicken or vegetable stock
- ☐ **Side:** cauliflower rice
- ☐ 6 cup(s) cauliflower rice

Sauces/Condiments

- ☐ 8 Tbsp olive oil
- ☐ 3 cup(s) salsa verde sauce

Spices

- ☐ 2 Tbsp minced onion
- ☐ 2 Tbsp ground cumin
- ☐ 4 tsp garlic powder
- ☐ Salt and pepper
- ☐ 2 packet(s) taco seasoning
- ☐ 4 garlic cloves
- ☐ 2 Tbsp Italian seasoning
- ☐ 2 tsp ground cumin

Dairy/Frozen

- ☐ 2 cup(s) shredded Monterrey Jack cheese
- ☐ **Garnish:** sour cream

Supplies

- ☐ **Side:** 10 gallon-size freezer baggie(s)

Freezer Meal Prep Day Shopping List by Recipe

Note: This shopping list doesn't include any side dish items like rice, dinner rolls, veggies or salad.
**In addition to a shopping list for prep day, this list could be used to help you organize ingredients on your counter before you begin preparing the meals for the freezer.

1. New Mexican Chicken Lettuce Wraps

- ☐ 6 large boneless chicken breasts
- ☐ 2 cup(s) red salsa
- ☐ 2 - 4 oz. can(s) green chiles
- ☐ 2 Tbsp minced onion
- ☐ 2 Tbsp ground cumin
- ☐ 2 tsp garlic powder
- ☐ Salt and pepper
- ☐ 2 gallon-size freezer baggie(s)

2. Paleo Chicken Taco Salad

- ☐ 2 green bell pepper(s)
- ☐ 2 orange bell pepper(s)
- ☐ 2 small white onion(s)
- ☐ 4 large boneless chicken breasts
- ☐ 1/2 cup(s) lime juice
- ☐ 2 packet(s) taco seasoning
- ☐ 2 gallon-size freezer baggie(s)

3. Paleo Minestrone Soup

- ☐ 4 Tbsp olive oil
- ☐ 2 small white onion(s)
- ☐ 4 celery
- ☐ 4 garlic cloves
- ☐ 8 whole carrots
- ☐ 1 lb(s) green beans
- ☐ 4 medium zucchini
- ☐ 2 - 15 oz. can(s) tomato sauce
- ☐ 2 Tbsp Italian seasoning
- ☐ 12 cup(s) chicken or vegetable stock
- ☐ Salt and pepper
- ☐ 2 gallon-size freezer baggie(s)

4. Slow Cooker Lemon & Dill Salmon

- ☐ 2 lb(s) salmon fillet
- ☐ Salt and pepper
- ☐ 4 tsp lemon juice
- ☐ 4 tsp fresh dill
- ☐ 2 gallon-size freezer baggie(s)

5. Slow Cooker Salsa Verde Shredded Pork

- ☐ 4 lb(s) pork shoulder roast
- ☐ 2 tsp garlic powder
- ☐ 2 tsp ground cumin
- ☐ Salt and pepper
- ☐ 3 cup(s) salsa verde sauce
- ☐ 2 large jalapeño(s)
- ☐ 2 gallon-size freezer baggie(s)

Freezer Meal Prep Day Shopping List by Store Section/Category

Note: This shopping list doesn't include any side dish items like fruit, dinner rolls, veggies or salad.

Meat

- ☐ 10 large boneless chicken breasts
- ☐ 2 lb(s) salmon fillet
- ☐ 4 lb(s) pork shoulder roast

Produce

- ☐ 2 green bell pepper(s)
- ☐ 2 orange bell pepper(s)
- ☐ 4 small white onion(s)
- ☐ 1/2 cup(s) lime juice
- ☐ 4 celery
- ☐ 8 whole carrots
- ☐ 1 lb(s) green beans
- ☐ 4 medium zucchini
- ☐ 4 tsp lemon juice
- ☐ 4 tsp fresh dill
- ☐ 2 large jalapeño(s)

Pantry Staples - Canned, Boxed

- ☐ 2 cup(s) red salsa
- ☐ 2 - 4 oz. can(s) green chiles
- ☐ 2 - 15 oz. can(s) tomato sauce
- ☐ 12 cup(s) chicken or vegetable stock

Sauces/Condiments

- ☐ 4 Tbsp olive oil
- ☐ 3 cup(s) salsa verde sauce

Spices

- ☐ 2 Tbsp minced onion
- ☐ 2 Tbsp ground cumin
- ☐ 4 tsp garlic powder
- ☐ Salt and pepper
- ☐ 2 packet(s) taco seasoning
- ☐ 4 garlic cloves
- ☐ 2 Tbsp Italian seasoning
- ☐ 2 tsp ground cumin

Supplies

- ☐ 10x gallon-size freezer baggie(s)

Meal Assembly Instructions

- ☐ Label your bags/foil with printable labels or sharpie.
- ☐ Pull out all the ingredients into a central location or into stations.

Pre-Cook & Chop Instructions

- ☐ Chop 2 white onions.
- ☐ Peel and chop 8 whole carrots.
- ☐ Slice 4 celery stalks.
- ☐ Trim 1 lb. green beans.
- ☐ Cut 2 lbs. salmon into 8 - 1/4 lb. fillets.
- ☐ Thinly slice 4 chicken breasts.
- ☐ Halve 4 lemons.
- ☐ Finely chop 4 tsp fresh dill.
- ☐ Seed and slice 2 green bell peppers and 2 red bell peppers. Slice 2 small white onions.
- ☐ Remove the seeds and dice 2 jalapenos.
- ☐ Thinly slice 4 medium zucchini.
- ☐ Open 2 cans of tomato sauce.

The Assembly Prep should take between 30 to 35 minutes.

Assembly by Recipe (Set Out on the Counter)

If you prefer to load your freezer baggies and trays one recipe at a time, you can follow the below instructions.

New Mexican Chicken Lettuce Wraps

To each gallon-size plastic freezer baggie, add the following ingredients:

- 3 large boneless chicken breasts
- 1 cup red salsa
- 1 - 4 oz. can green chiles
- 1 Tbsp minced onion
- 1 Tbsp ground cumin
- 1 tsp garlic powder
- Salt and pepper

Remove as much air as possible and seal. Add label to baggie and freeze.

Paleo Chicken Taco Salad

To each gallon-size plastic freezer baggie, add the following ingredients:

- Half of the sliced chicken breasts
- Half of the sliced green bell peppers
- Half of the sliced red bell peppers
- Half of the sliced onion
- 1/4 cup lime juice
- 1 packet taco seasoning

Remove as much air as you can and seal. Freeze up to 6 months in your fridge freezer or 12 months in a deep freezer.

Paleo Minestrone Soup

To each gallon-size plastic freezer baggie, add the following ingredients:

- Half of the chopped onion
- Half of the chopped celery
- 2 garlic cloves, crushed
- Half of the chopped carrots
- Half of the trimmed green beans
- Half of the sliced zucchini

- 1 - 15 oz. can tomato sauce
- 1 Tbsp Italian seasoning blend
- 6 cups chicken or vegetable stock

Remove as much air as possible and seal. Add label to baggie and freeze.

Slow Cooker Lemon & Dill Salmon

To each gallon-size plastic freezer baggie, add the following ingredients:

- Half of the salmon fillets
- Salt and pepper
- Juice from 2 lemons
- Half of the chopped dill

Remove as much air as possible and seal. Add label to baggie and freeze.

Slow Cooker Salsa Verde Shredded Pork

To each gallon-size plastic freezer baggie, add the following ingredients:

- 2 lb. pork shoulder roast
- 1 tsp garlic powder
- 1 tsp ground cumin
- Salt and pepper
- 1 1/2 cups salsa verde sauce
- Half of the diced jalapeno into each bag

Remove as much air as possible and seal. Add label to baggie and freeze.

Freezer Cooking Resources
from Erin Chase

Let's Connect

Hi friend! Need more help or inspiration on your f reezer cooking journey? Come join our group on Facebook - it's basically a "freezer cooking hotline" and an amazing, supportive community.
Visit https://bit.ly/MyFrEZFB to join the group.

Join MyFreezEasy

Freezer Meal Cookbooks

Freezer Meal Plan PDFs

Made in the USA
Middletown, DE
25 September 2023

39355880R00060